I Can Publish the Pirate Way

Pirate Publishing
In the Era of the Information Dealer

David Mark Brown

I Say Publish the Pirate Way: Pirate Publishing in the Era of the Information Dealer
By David Mark Brown

This book is the opinions of David Mark Brown. While a work of nonfiction, names, descriptions, entities, and incidents included in this book are subject to the author's interpretation. Everything is meant in a respectful manner.

ISBN: 978-1-947655-56-0
Published by Fiction Vortex, Inc. (FV Press)
Nampa, ID 83651
http://www.fictionvortex.com

Cover Art by Niels Christensen; design by DMB
Published in the United States of America

To all the Pirate Authors filling in the map

of the Information High Seas.

A Confession From the Author

I don't know if this is really a confession, but it feels like one. I'm an oddball, and life is hard for us oddballs. It's especially hard when you're committed to making life better for all the oddballs. No oddball left behind. This is my commitment. It woke me up at 4am this morning. I believe it can be done, if we do it together.

After growing up as a redneck on a cattle ranch in Texas, I graduated as a granola from the University of Montana with high honors and an Elementary Education degree.

I then spent thirteen years developing world-changers at Boise State University and the University of Utah. I poured thousands of hours into students who have gone on to do amazing things, and will do many more yet.

Working with young people has allowed me to remain in a constant state of hope and belief. I've yet to have my dreams beat out of me. I still believe we can make the world a better place.

I left this former life because there was still something left undone, something I needed to do on a larger scale. But I needed all the lessons along the way to survive the effort.

And so here we are. The last eight years have been about building the foundation for a unique community of oddballs who still believe they can make the world a better place. I think you're one of those oddballs. Storytellers have a mighty power to shape humanity. We know this to be true! It has been true in your own life, so don't doubt your ability to have the same impact on others!

We now need this power to be focused and deployed strategically in a manner that improves critical thinking and expands empathy across the human race. I think you have a part to play in this, and so I'm asking for a favor. Consider committing to the Pirate Author Code. That's an easy one compared to what I'm about to ask next.

I'm also asking that you consider joining the community on location at the next nearest S3 (StoryShop Summit) event. I know. This is a huge ask. It will cost a lot of money. (If finances are the only obstacle, reach out to me via email.) We wouldn't go through all the tremendous work required to host these live gatherings if we didn't think them critical to the community.

To accomplish the ridiculous task in front of us (inspiring a mentally, emotionally, and spiritually healthier human race), we'll need to meet each other. We'll need to deepen our relationships. We'll need to share our inspiration in person. Then, together, we'll set about writing the stories and building the tools necessary to restore reading to relevancy for ourselves and our children...one oddball at a time. (It's about getting your stories into the hands of the oddballs who need it the most right at the critical time they need it!)

I deeply thank you for taking the time to read this. I'm grateful for the community we've built so far--for all the oddballs. You're important, and you're important to me.

David Mark Brown
Pirate Captain

Part I: The PAC

Chapter One

The Pirate Author Code

Why all the romanticizing of pirates, you may ask. Aarrrr, that's a downright necessary question. After all, historically, most of these chaps were (and still are) ruthless scoundrels quite willing to (if I may quote a classic movie) "Burn the village! and rape the horses! and ride off on the women! and uh, plunder! and uh...prune...the hedges...of many small villages!"

To be perfectly clear, this is NOT what I am proposing we authors do within the publishing oceans. So what *do* I mean by Pirate Author, and by extension, Pirate Publishing?

As was the case in the golden era of sailing the high seas, today's publishing oceans are fraught with chaos (information dealers) and rival powers (information brokers) attempting to stake claim to the storytelling commerce and richness of content (our personal narratives) sailing the vastness of these publishing oceans (information distribution network).

Allow me to explain...no, there is too much. Allow me first to sum up.

We Live During the Era of the Information Dealer

At one point, the high seas were circumnavigated by the spice dealers. Then we evolved into slave dealers. Then arms and munitions dealers. Welcome to the era of the information dealer as the Ruler Supreme of the high seas. Pick your information dealer du jour. We've got the grifty-domestic flavor, the disenfranchised Macedonian lot, or the Russian Web brigades.

Just as the arms dealers and profiteers of the past stirred up murder and chaos for the purpose of profit, so too the information dealers pander to the lowest common denominator for the purpose of profit. Their weapons of choice are link-bait, fake news, click farms, and spammy content.

The golden era of the information dealer has been ushered in via the sudden rise of large information brokers. The largest brokers are companies like AT&T, Amazon, Facebook, News Corp, and Google. The brokers have arisen due to the blossoming of the digital frontier—an expanse of digital real estate based on our personal narratives that most of us don't think about or perceive by the same set of rules that the information brokers do.

The information dealers utilize the platforms and structures built by the brokers to turn a quick and dirty profit. This utilization creates a quiet, symbiotic relationship between the brokers and the dealers at the expense of the rest of us. Only when the abuse by the dealers grows too rampant does it harm the bottom line of the broker (by pissing off regular folk until we change our online behavior).

Not all digital marketers are information dealers, and there are obviously still legitimate uses for digital advertising and marketing. But the industry has become so deluged with bilge and bad actors that even widely accepted practices have become manipulative in an effort to scratch out a better return on investment (ROI) in the face of a tidal wave of outright immoral practices.

At this point, I recommend you check out the YouTube video, "The Good Fight Short: Russian Troll Farm" if you haven't seen it. It's just 1:19 long. I'll wait.

These bad actors are the information dealers.

One report[i] claims that during 2018 digital advertisers wasted $51,000,000 a DAY on fraudulent ads (i.e., ads that displayed on spammy and fraudulent sites created by information dealers for nothing more than generating clicks and getting paid for the ads displayed). From what I can tell, that doesn't even include much of the low-quality, polarizing rhetoric barfed into the digital ecosystem to keep all us chattel on edge enough to deplete our bank accounts on temporary solutions or to vote yes on proposition 24. ("Will someone please think of the children!")

These information dealers have co-opted our stories (our personal information is our story), commodified them, and weaponized them in their successful efforts to stir up fear and hatred for the purpose of profit. This affects writers directly, because Amazon is an emerging favorite target for information dealers (i.e., page-stuffing, fake reviews, click farms, fake books, plagiarism, thinly-veiled rhetoric, and straight-up garbage writing). And with Amazon being THE behemoth in publishing, its deteriorating trustworthiness has the potential to tank the livelihoods of thousands of authors (see YouTube as a recent example[ii]).

Avail ye of the Pirate Author Code, all ye pirates!

Okay, so I'm trying to make a colorful analogy à la Pirates of the Caribbean, you know, in an attempt to make the point more memorable, marketable, and viral. Anywho, let's all channel our best Captain Jack.

Pirate Authors differentiate ourselves from information dealers in five distinct ways. These five differentiators are the core of the five tenets of the Pirate Author Code.

> *Pirate Authors are all about 1.) increasing reader engagement by 2.) increasing brand assets via 3.) brand loyalty tactics with 4.) increased collaboration that combine to 5.) promote an abundance mindset.*

All of this abundance leads to empathy and critical thinking, and that's the end goal of Pirate Authors. (Here is where I'll spare you my rant on how reading is vital to us connecting with others and interpreting the world around us, and how without quality narrative fiction we as a civilization are racing toward our ghettoized doom.)

> *In direct contrast with Pirate Authors, information dealers choose to 1.) increase reader conversion by 2.) eroding brand assets via 3.) brand friction tactics that 4.) increase isolation and combine to 5.) promote a scarcity mindset.*

Scarcity leads to fear and hatred. These are the consequences of the information dealers.

The Code is not a formula.

These five tenets are not the five steps toward success. There is no treasure map to riches. There is no easy life for Pirates. Not until our code is adapted far enough and wide enough to reshape the storytelling industry into something that punishes information dealers and relegate brokers to their appropriate places. (See the call to action at the end of this.)

In general, formulas (like "The secrets that Adsense doesn't want you to know!" or "How to 10x your Amazon ad revenues!") work less and less effectively as more people learn about them and implement them. Formulas are driven by scarcity.

The beauty of a Code is that it becomes more effective and more powerful as more people commit to it. Codes are driven by abundance. The broader we spread the message, the greater and deeper the impact Pirate Publishing will have on our beloved industry of storytelling.

It's time to take back the high seas of publishing. Without further ado, here are the five tenets of the "Pirate Author Code."

1) Pirate Authors are beholden to reader engagement. (Engagement Vs. Conversion)

We've been set up to fail because we've been tricked to gauge our success by the wrong metrics. The metrics we've been spoon-fed are for tracking consumer conversions rather than reader engagement.

"What's the big diff?" you may ask...if you grew up in the eighties. Well, my fellow Generation Xer, the big diff is that conversion gauges the effectiveness of your marketing package. Engagement gauges the effectiveness of your storytelling. Which is a better indicator of your success as an author? (Hint, the answer is engagement.)

I hate to be the one to tell you this, and by "hate" I mean "relish," but if you are generating written content and you are concerned about conversion at the expense of engagement, you are an information dealer concerned about quick payouts via spammy content over quality storytelling. (Oofah!)

I'm not saying you shouldn't be concerned about conversion. Of course, you can't engage a reader unless you first convert that reader as a consumer. But Pirate Authors understand that conversion metrics such as reviews, rankings, and royalties are for evaluating the effectiveness of marketing success and not author success.

For evaluating success as a writer, Pirate Authors rely on metrics such as read-through and direct call-to-action click-through (i.e., ask people to do something and track the percentage of them that do it). These metrics can tell you how much a reader is engaged with your author brand. Now that you have an author brand, it's time to protect it.

2) Pirate Authors cover their assets.
(Author Brand Vs. Broker Brand)

This is one of those things we have to hold as an ideal while accepting that our reality ain't gonna reach that ideal much of the time. But hey, pirates should be comfortable with shades of grey. Some trade-offs are absolutely worth it. That doesn't mean we shouldn't dream of a perfect world where those trade-offs aren't necessary.

Maintaining **ownership** of assets comes into play more with contracts and traditional publishing, but we need to be mindful of ownership when signing with Audible and other platforms as well. Pirate Authors spend time understanding rights and intellectual property.

Control of assets deals with the two-sided coin of distribution and discoverability and includes such things as pricing, exposure, exclusivity, DRM, meta-data, and branding. As with ownership, there may be times that giving over control is worth the value you're getting in return.

Access overlaps with ownership and control but differs enough to be mentioned separately. Think of access as the amount of information and data pertaining to your assets that you are given...well, access to. Do you know the names or emails of your readers? Are you allowed to contact them?

As writers, we spend our creative lives making assets. If commercialized, those assets will belong to someone. That someone will most likely be us or an information broker (or both). Pirate Authors fight to maintain as much ownership, control, and access to their assets as feasible in order to emphasize their author brand over broker brands as much as possible.

3) Pirate Authors grow brand loyalty.
(Loyalty Vs. Friction)

This tenet is less about who owns the brand and more about the methods used to grow the brand. StoryShop has an internal policy known as "Trips Neg D." (See chapter sixteen.) This moniker is short for "Don't be a dick, douche, or dumbass." We're quite serious about this policy as a guiding force on all of our relationships and business practices. Anything less will generate friction between us and our audience.

The same goes for Pirate Authors. If brand loyalty is what you want, then don't be a dick. That's what information dealers are all about. If a marketing tactic feels sleazy to you, then find something more authentic to your brand.

Paid advertising is friction. This friction can be mitigated when advertising is done well, but it will always be friction.

I hear the masses crying out, "How the hell am I supposed to market my content without paid advertising!?" I'm not insisting we abandon paid ads. In the current market, it is next to impossible to find traction without them. Pirate

Authors must be mindful of the friction these ads generate for their readers in order to maintain a higher ledger of loyalty.

In addition to the innate friction generated by legitimate ads, the increasing abuse of paid advertising by information dealers will increase this friction, which will in turn lead to diminishing returns for legitimate ads. So to sum up, expect increasing friction and diminishing returns from any paid advertising system.

All of this is the reason why Pirate Authors should not abandon tried-and-true methods of loyalty marketing and traction building. When done well, email marketing, content marketing, and community building generate loyalty. Popular examples include thought leaders such as Seth Godin and Tim Ferriss and companies such as Patagonia and Zappos. Connect readers with your author brand and provide them value on a regular basis.

4) Pirate Authors sail as a Pirate Crew.
(Collaboration Vs. Isolation)

While a pirate I be, it's not the lonely life for me. I draw within myself when I put words to the page, but I don't create content in a relational vacuum. I need my pirate crew. I think we all do. Storytelling is a collaborative process. The richer our relationships, and the richer our collaborations, the richer our stories will be.

On top of it all, the result of being constantly assaulted by information dealers is isolation. We are being prodded and provoked into "us vs. them" groupings in order to be targeted more efficiently by adverts. Reading and writing needs to bring us together. The only "us vs. them" we should acknowledge is Pirate Authors vs. Information Dealers.

Pirate Authors are intentional to sail as part of a crew. Support each other. Invest in each other.

5) Pirate Authors support the broader Pirate Community. (Abundance Vs. Scarcity)

Pirate Authors live out of a world-view based on abundance. Creativity itself insists on a foundation of abundance. By snatching words or images out of the air, do we deplete the available stock of creativity? Preposterous!

By shaping words into story, we make the world richer. And the more those stories are shared, the richer we all become! The more people start to read, the more those people want to finish reading. Reading begets more reading. The higher the quality of the reading, the more people want to read. The more relevant the reading delivery vehicle, the more people want to read.

For the time being, paid advertising pits us against each other (as we attempt to outbid each other for eyeballs), while also adding friction to the reader's experience. But our competition is not other authors. It isn't other books. We can't write more than people can read. We are competing against other forms of digital media and entertainment. We are competing with mobile apps and social media. The more we combine our writerly efforts to bring reading back to relevancy, the more all of us win. The more humanity wins.

Our only enemies are the information dealers with their efforts to tear down our industry by pumping it full of bilge and by polluting our readers' expectations and trust.

To succeed over the long-term, the publishing industry must find a means to connect the abundant creativity of storytelling with our abundant audience without brokering the connection with an ecosystem built on a foundation of competition and scarcity.

Between now and then, Pirate Authors will counter the brokers and the dealers by refusing to be isolated. By fostering community, we will pioneer a solution.

The Future Promise of the Pirate Author Code (The Call to Proliferation!)

Together, as Pirate Authors, we can force a better future. We can take back the high seas from the dealers who would profit on human division and fear-mongering. We can craft stories that entertain, inform, and empower. We can advocate for and incentivize the emergence of a platform driven by connectivity and empathy rather than competitive ad spend and the bottom dollar.

These are the goals of the Pirate Author. There are two possible ways by which we will accomplish them. When our numbers swell to the tipping point we will either 1) spur the necessary changes or 2) orchestrate them ourselves.

But to achieve this goal of prompting or building a platform that connects readers with writers according to the five tenets of the Pirate Author Code, we must swell the ranks of those who would profess allegiance to the Code!

To do so, we ask that Pirate Authors first pledge allegiance to the Code by adding their email to the form located here: *https://university.storyshop.io/pirate-author-code/*.

Second, we ask that Pirate Authors spread the word about the Pirate Author Code by using the free tool available at our website to generate the watermark of the Pirate Author on any and all visuals used for marketing your content and / or brand. When possible, link interested authors back to our website. And use one of our hashtags to help connect your comments with the community: #JoinTheStory, #PirateAuthor, #PiratePublishing.

Power to the Pirate Author.

Part II: The Seascape

CHAPTER TWO

INFORMATION BROKERS, FUTURE OWNERS?

We are playing a dangerous game, all of us, whether we realize it or not. I'm gonna go beyond the scope of publishing for the next few chapters in order to address the entirety of the "information distribution network" of which we are inescapably entangled as content consumers as well as content creators. Try not to become too disturbed by the following content, à la "Adam Ruins Everything.[iii]"

How does the following sound as far as a fun game night? Start off by gathering together with a mixture of friends and strangers at a large "game bar" where you self-select loose groups. You're prompted to get to know each other by sharing what superhero power you want and by discussing the next tattoo you're gonna get...oh, and possible games to play.

You're then prompted to relocate to more specific "gaming rooms" according to your answers. You hit it off with these new people who like the same games as you (and don't have stupid tattoo ideas). During the course of the conversation you naturally find yourself making fun of the other game groups. I mean, *The Lego Movie* was fine and all, but a tattoo of Unikitty?

These games, in the more specific game room, really connect with you. You buy one. You plan another game night with your new "us" group. You go home.

This process should seem familiar. It's what is done to us continuously...digitally, and it's not particularly heinous when taken one instance at a time. But after dozens of instances everyday, we start to feel paranoid about all those "other" people out there who simply aren't like "us."

Make no mistake, we ARE participants whether we are active or passive in the game. Our entire online experience is being sorted and filtered. The results of our queries, the ads and links we see, the stories in our feeds—all of it has been tailored to prompt us toward certain decisions and actions that are driven by a motivation for profit.

Welcome to your new "us" groups.

One of the unfortunate side-effects of this "dangerous game" for society is ghettoization. Stratification. Call it what you like. Classifying us makes us easier to target with specific calls to action. Based on active and passive feedback, we are grouped with others like us so that fear, anger, and lust triggers can be optimized to prompt our desired behavior. (Fear and Hatred drive ROI better than more nuanced emotions. As we know, enragement is engagement!)

I mean, holy crap, man. Fathom that for just a second...

Your generation, your ethnicity, your orientation, your politics, your religious views, your habits, your tastes...have you shaped these things? Or are they shaping you? Because in any area where you are not actively shaping and defining yourself, information brokers are. They know if you shade toward liberal compassion. They know if you tend to buy impulse, indulgence items late at night. They know if you favor the NFL or the players union when it comes to anthem protests.

The brokers aren't pulling your strings directly. The information dealers are doing that. The brokers control access to your narrative. The brokers pave the way for the dealers to pour fuel on your fire and then profit from your emotional responses.

This is a side note in relation to explaining who the information brokers are, but I challenge us all to actively consider the "us vs. them" groups we find ourselves in. Did you even realize you were in so many? Out of state drivers? Conservatives? Gun nuts? Religious wackos? Seahawks fans? Smokers? Teetotalers? Urban hipsters? Baby Boomers? The entitled? The fat? The gym rats? Inoculation conspirators? Plastic diaper users? We can be fanned into hatred for anyone! And information dealers are reaping the profits.

Right now I'm getting pissed at those urban truck owners who somehow think parking across two to three spots will keep me from crowding too close to their precious paint job and dinging it with my neutrally painted, sensibly-sized hybrid vehicle! Damn you! Damn you all to hell! (Now where's my CBD oil to soothe this mongo headache? Oh, damn, I need a new bottle.)

Ehem, still doubt that we're being isolated and segregated? Okay, let's push on.

Defining the Roles: Information Brokers

There are three well-defined roles to play in the information distribution network. I advocate for a fourth.

The established three roles are brokers, dealers, and pawns. I advocate for content creators to band together as

Pirate Authors in pirate crews. But for this post, we'll stick with understanding the brokers.

Information Brokers: These are the organizations (typically large corporations) at the top of the power structure. The most powerful brokers today (2019) are Google, Facebook, AT&T, and Amazon. The brokers own the infrastructure that make the trades possible. They are profit-driven entities who tend to flow toward profit opportunities like water flows downhill. They are more amoral than immoral.

The large brokers are also constantly at war with each other over controlling access to new possible forms of information and data. Sometimes these battles play out more visibly, such as Google's recent attempts[iv] to improve their own commerce solution rather than sending their searches to Amazon for the final purchase.

The digital revolution has opened up a new frontier of valuable digital property. Similar to the Homestead Act of 1862, or the Oklahoma Land Rush of 1893, there is a sense of romanticism, greed, and entitlement over property that isn't exactly "free and clear." The frontier lands were host to plenty of residents who, unfortunately for them, didn't share the same concept of ownership as the pioneers.

Welcome to the digital frontier (not the desert of the real). The digital frontier consists of our personal data, our intellectual property, and digital records and facsimiles created from our physical assets. This frontier is so new that ownership over these things is sketchy at best. Like the First Peoples of North America, the current residents of the digital frontier don't share the same concept of digital property ownership as the information brokers do. In lies the opportunity for the brokers. (This stuff really is strikingly reminiscent of Fishburne explaining the Matrix.)

Here is a recent development in the digital frontier that will serve as an adequately creepy example of why we should restructure the way we think about our digital information before it's too late. Most of you have probably seen advertisements for some sort of video doorbell. Amazon has acquired the Ring Video Doorbell, and has begun promoting it pretty heavily. They've actually teamed up with police departments[v] to promote the implementation of the technology as a method to fight crime.

On the surface, this seems like a great way to use technology to keep us safer. But who will own the video recorded by video doorbells? Currently, if you opt to share data with the police, they can use that data for any purpose they choose (not just the case in question), keep that data forever, and share that data with other government agencies. What will Amazon ultimately decide to do with the data? And how many times will they change the terms of service without you noticing?

The possibilities are endless. How valuable would it be to have an extensive facial recognition database? I can think of several uses for information based on the pedestrian and auto-traffic passing in front of my home. Who should own this information? And why shouldn't I have the option to be compensated for its usefulness? This is just one example of the massive opportunities that brokers are driven by.

Brokers are smart and they see the big picture. Outright ownership of the data/content of the digital frontier is difficult, time consuming, expensive, and likely to be legally problematic down the road. And in the case of some intellectual property, laws already exist.

Chokepoints are critical for brokers.

Brokers look for chokepoints to control. Chokepoints are the equivalent of strategic assets such as fresh-water springs, river fords, safe harbors, and the narrow passageway defended by Leonidas and the 300 Spartans in the film 300. Control a digital chokepoint and you can set your price for access to the asset on the other side. The need to preserve these digital chokepoints is the fundamental reason why net neutrality was revoked and is still under assault from large information brokers who have plenty of money to lobby Congress. But that is a post for another day.

Each of the large brokers has locked down at least one major chokepoint, and they leverage that chokepoint to gain others or to expand current ones. Amazon is where we go to buy things, including my precious CBD oil. Facebook is where we go to share things, like photos of over-sized urban trucks parked across three spaces!!! Google is where we go to find things, like hybrid vehicle support groups. AT&T is how we access the internet. (Now why won't this support group page open?...)

Uhhh, think about that last one for a minute. Which company controls your access to the internet? That's a key chokepoint. What happens if that company decides to bludgeon a competitor by slowing down access to their competitor's content? Or by removing shortcuts from its dashboard? Or by dropping access to certain content altogether? This is happening right now with Direct TV (AT&T).[vi]

Where do we go from here?

Anyway, those are the brokers. There is no escaping them. We need to be aware of how they operate, and we need to be aware of the digital frontier they are attempting to control.

By being educated on the matter, we can push back when the brokers attempt to make digital land grabs[vii]. By educating ourselves and others, we can reduce the societal impacts or the "us vs. them" impacts of the fear mongering that the brokers enable.

This leads us into the discussion about the information dealers. There is a sort of bright side to all of this, but we've gotta go deeper in before we come out the other side. Endurance. Endurance, I say!

Chapter Three

Information Dealers, Chaos Reapers

In the last chapter, we dug into the identity and objectives of the information brokers. Now it's time to drill down on the "Dealers." Just who are these mysterious individuals who do such a craptastic job of delivering all the muck that's fit to rake? And how are these people affecting the publishing high seas?

First off, a disclaimer. It's fun (or at least simple) to profile and stereotype. That's the reason we all do it, whether we intend to or not. For educational purposes, I'm going to openly engage in creating a few information dealer profiles. This by no means indicates that I believe everyone who falls into these profiles is a smarmy information dealer. So don't be a douche about it. Pretty please?

What's the definition of an information dealer? Anyone who is employed or employs others with the primary purpose of generating and propagating sensationalized content that maximizes ratings, clicks, and/or profit with an open disregard for validity.

Who are the Information Dealers?

If you haven't read about the city of Veles in Macedonia, CNN has a solid read[viii] about how an entire city is revitalizing its devastated economy by pumping fake news into the United States. On one level, this is ingenious, and I totally get it. I mean, screw America and its pretentious ways, am I right? [wink, wink.]

If you've seen the movie, *Team America: World Police*, this is where you should be humming the theme music to yourself. If you haven't seen it, I can't openly recommend it. Doing so might get me blacklisted even more than I already am...but I kid (not really). The movie is terrible. (It's hilarious.)

I spent the summers of 1996 and 1997 in Ukraine (not THE Ukraine, for the love of Gorbachev; they hate that). I also spent time in Turkey during the travel ban weeks after 9-11. I'm from Texas, officially the most offensive state in the United States (as far as loudmouthed international travelers go). I'm aware of how the rest of the planet struggles with their relationship with us. The simple fact that we've co-opted the term "Americans," even though we're from only one of the countries in North America is pretty pretentious.

So it doesn't surprise me that the mayor of Veles has been quoted saying, "We don't even try to stop them" in regards to the entrepreneurs engaged in generating fake news for the American consumer public. Along those lines, meet the first information dealer profile.

Information Dealer Profile #1: Disenfranchised Macedonians

A growing legion of disenfranchised young people in Macedonia are spewing fake news into our society for more money in a day than they could otherwise make in six months. If given the choice of drugs, prostitution, or fake news...I gotta admit, fake news would be a no-brainer for me. I'd be right there generating stories about how Trump flew into a rage over democrats claiming he was signing a deal to become the next big erectile dysfunction spokesperson.

It's hard for me to hate these people. Yet the damage on our society is real and intensifying.

Information Dealer Profile #2: The Russian Web Brigades

For a second profile on information dealers, let's travel to Mother Russia. Yep, here is where we mention the Russian Web Brigades[ix]. This is where the 2016 presidential elections and Facebook become intricately interwoven into the saga. The key differences between these web brigades and the entrepreneurs of Macedonia are their motivations. Russian motivations are primarily political while the motivations of the Macedonians are primarily monetary.

Russian efforts are centralized and organized, while the Macedonians are only loosely-organized, independent dealers. In the end, the Russian Brigades are still composed of individuals trying to improve their position in life.

Ironically, the content produced is often similar. (Turns out that the American political circus is a top money-maker. Who would have thunk it.)

Information Dealer Profile #3: Domestic Freelancers

Lest I look like some sort of foreigner basher, let's turn the focus inward for the final profile[x]. It turns out citizens of the ole' US of A also like turning a fast buck. There are plenty of domestic content providers maximizing profits from spinning sensational polemic via websites, YouTube, podcasts, and radio. While politics is the easiest place to dig up information dealers from both extremes, topics such as race, religion, and orientation also generate ample fodder for information dealers.

When it comes to these domestic information dealers, some of them should be classified as ideologues, meaning they believe in their extreme rhetoric. The rest simply recognize there is money to be made from clickbait articles and media. Some rather large celebrity personalities in the United States should be considered nothing more than information dealers due to the fact that they appear to care about ratings, clicks, and profit far above the validity or value of their content. This is, after all, the definition of an information dealer (at least according to me, and I'm the one writing this book).

How do information dealers make money?

Despite all the hubbub surrounding Facebook and the 2016 presidential elections, Brother Zuck and his international platform (that some people are starting to refer to as a surveillance platform rather than social media) isn't the magic sauce for information dealers. It turns out that Google's AdSense is. Or in a more general sense, digital advertising services are the magic sauce.

Information dealers make the vast majority of their money from the ad revenue their content generates. So while it's true that information dealers utilize Facebook to find readers, they profit by sending those readers off of Facebook and onto platforms that allow them to generate ad money based on clicks/views.

Google's AdSense is by far the largest advertising service and therefore has the highest profit-generating potential for information dealers. These information dealer's frequent and heavy usage of AdSense is why a study[xi] among digital advertisers in 2018 claimed that legitimate agencies and individuals purchasing ad space through AdSense were wasting 51 million dollars a day. In other words, during 2018 it was estimated that 51 million dollars a day went into the pockets of information dealers whose fake news sites were displaying legitimate ads. If you've spent digital ad money in the last few years, it's guaranteed that some of it was paid out to information dealers.

How does this play out for the publishing industry?
The key piece to keep in mind is that information dealers need a platform with ads to make money. YouTube, as an example, went through a massive upheaval a couple years ago (2017) when major sponsors threatened to yank their advertising dollars if their advertising spots continued to be played before scandalous or sensational content. Thousands of profitable, legitimate YouTubers were caught up in the collateral damage when their content was demonetized almost overnight.

The second thing to keep in mind is that platforms are continually doing stuff like YouTube did (with all the grace of unlicensed surgeon, Moe Sizlack) in an attempt to block information dealers once the pain point gets too high. This leads to information dealers doing one of two things: either they find a new way to slip past the platform's efforts to block them, or they find a new platform to infiltrate—one less equipped to stop them and one less inundated by other information dealers.

Enter Amazon. Yep, Amazon is now fully immersed in the highly-profitable space of digital ads. And double yep, Amazon has nowhere near the experience that Google and Facebook have in countering the efforts of information dealers. Triple yep, Amazon has become a new target of information dealers.

We've seen early attempts to gamify Kindle Unlimited via page-stuffing and click farm borrows. We've seen mass, fake reviews. For each of these hacks, Amazon has demonstrated clumsy follow-up / cover-up skills that make Facebook look darn-right svelte. For a couple of years now, people have complained about Amazon Marketplace (their space for Third Party Sellers) being out of control and overrun with shysters.

Despite the dangers, the potential profit is too great to resist. Amazon has launched its Onsite Associates program[xii] (invitation only at this point) as another step toward allowing monetized-marketing content onto its platform.

Each of these is a lever for information dealers to pull in order to make money at the expense of readers and legitimate writers: reviews, KU read through, top 100 lists, monetized product guides, Amazon Marketplace, sponsored product ads, and product display ads.

It goes without saying that Amazon is the largest information broker for the publishing industry. It also goes without saying that Amazon's primary markets are not publishing. The combination of these two things should have writers soiling their armor whenever they think about the future of their beloved industry.

What the [bleep] can we do about information dealers?
Much like the information brokers, it's next to impossible to avoid the information dealers. They swim and breathe in the same digital waters that we traverse on a daily basis. I admit the present looks grim, but the future of publishing could still be very bright.

The impact of information dealers has gone largely unnoticed by most fiction readers. While the "all-you-can-read" buffet of Kindle Unlimited is negatively impacting reader's behavior and expectations, we are only one successful-alternative-platform away from revitalizing digital, narrative fiction.

In the meantime, there are things we Pirate Authors can do. We will discuss these possible solutions starting in chapter ten. Keep your eyes on the horizon, all ye Pirate Authors! We will get there!

Chapter Four

Pawns, It's Worse Than I Think

This gets dicey, and the content in this chapter might not be for everyone. Knowing stuff can make life less fun sometimes, and if you're the kind of person that can't learn something and then just "meh" it off when there's not much you can do about it, perhaps you should skip forward to the next chapter. As we used to say back in my university days, "duh is awe" sometimes. (We also used to say stuff like, Booyah! Totally banging, home-skillet.)

Big Brother, Big Data

Our favorite Big Data information brokers are increasingly acting with impunity these days. Their public behavior sorta makes me wonder if boardroom conversations are going something like this:

Executive Dude: "Oh, oh, wouldn't it be awesome if we could do this?"

Executive Dudette: "Don't you think people might object to us filming their intimate moments?"

Executive Dude: "Yeah, but then we use the data to create these little dancing emojis!"

Executive Dudette: "Oh, that's kick ass! Everyone's going to love it!"

Executive Dude: "Booyah, home-skillet!"

We have to partially blame ourselves. The public's past objections to the increasingly common data-grabs and privacy invasions have all too often been more "meh" than "holy-sheepskin, Batman!" And as it turns out, we love our dancing emojis.

There's no possible way to delve into all of the irrational hubris and overreaching that happens on the digital frontier. It will have to suffice to highlight a couple of recent examples.

One of the creepiest aspects of the new digital frontier is that so much of our personal information is being used in so many ways we know nothing about. This is the underlying reason for the ACLU's recent legal suit against the FBI over their use of facial recognition technology. Massive databases have been put together over the years via the Department of Motor Vehicles and other government departments. There is no consistent set of rules around what happens with these images, what they can be used for, or who they can be shared with.

Companies like Amazon and Microsoft have been selling facial recognition technologies[xiii] to other companies for quite some time. Heck, Amazon even offers its facial recognition capabilities to government agencies interested in running extensive scans on databases full of people who never consented to their faces being used in any such manner.

Why not? The information is already stored via Amazon Web Services. And Amazon's infrastructure is already set up to sort and filter the data. The only "Why not?" I can think of is that when I had my photo snapped for my driver's license no one asked me if I wanted it to be used to map my movements around town.

In other news, Google was recently busted[xiv] for hiring outside contractors to target homeless, black people for the purpose of improving facial recognition capabilities on the Pixel 4 phone. I imagine their confused response when confronted on the matter went something like the following.

Executive Dude: "What? Black people use smartphones, right?"

Journalist: "So the ends justify the means?"

Executive Dude: "I don't know what that means. But, you've heard about how crappy the iPhone's facial recognition is for dark faces, right? I mean, it's a gaping vulnerability large enough to drive truckloads of cash through."

Journalist: "Many see this as a callous move to profit off of a vulnerable and historically victimized populous."

Executive Dude: "As if! Don't be such a fart-knocker. We improved dark-face recognition by like 280%! Booyah! We're like the successors to MLKJ!"

Journalist: [shakes head, starts to object but then walks away]

Executive Dude: "Don't leave me hanging. Our launch party is gonna get crunk tonight!"

But wait! It gets better. And by better, I mean much worse. It turns out that about a third of the major websites we frequent are using shady digital fingerprint practices[xv] to identify, profile, and target us. This old-school capability is becoming more common at the same time new-fangled security measures are popping up to supposedly protect us from this sort of violation.

Uncle Sam ain't gonna come to the rescue.

This stuff is terrible, but at least we can trust the government to have our back, right? Uhh...sure. You just plug your ears and close your eyes for this next section. Well, you don't have to plug your ears unless you're listening to this outloud.

It turns out the deluge of comments that poured into the FCC expressing disdain for net neutrality and all of its egalitarian, freedom-loving, playing-field-leveling qualities were fabricated by a scourolous marketing firm[xvi] hired by, drumroll please...the FCC. Oh snap. You mean, government agencies cheat and lie? Well butter my biscuits. What is an honest citizen to do?

The Good News Bit

The good news is that there are a few things we can do. First off, don't be a dupe. If you are reading this, you're clearly of sound mind and...well, I can't deduce anything about your body. But, you're on the right track.

Find a few solid sources of news and information. I'm not going to give you a list, because the last thing we need right now is a bunch of DMB clones running around. Besides, I'm a bit of a podcast guy when it comes to news. You know, stuff like The Creative Penn, Reset, The Bad

Crypto Podcast, and the Sell More Book Show. For all I know, you might prefer print.

And if I told you I was a bit of a public radio wonk, you might judge me. If I paraded my frequenting of Wikipedia, I'd surely earn several big frowny-faces. Besides, anyone with a connected device and a clicky-finger could track my many references in this book to sites like David Gaughran's, Bo Sacks, C-Net, Digiday, and Buzzfeed. So the last thing I would do is give you a laundry list of sources I like. Go find your own!

Make sure your sources aren't all coming from the same bent. If you are an early adapter, be intentional to educate yourself on the new technologies, especially if those technologies generate or intersect big data. If the tech is connected to the information distribution network, be aware of what information is being trafficked and who has access to it. What, if any, rules are regulating its use? Does the information expire at some point or can it be stored indefinitely? Can it be shared with other organizations or companies?

And it never hurts to make a habit of saying stuff outloud like, "I respect and welcome our Amazon overlords." You know, just incase someone is listening in. I'm pretty sure the repeating of this exact phrase on a daily basis is what resulted in a really nice fruit and muffin basket being delivered to my house anonymously by drone last April. The card just said, "We appreciate your allegiance," and it was signed "your pal, Z-lord." Weird, right?

Brave Browser deserves a bolded header right about here. More good news, there are companies creating solutions. I've recently made the conversion on my computers and devices to Brave browser[xvii]. If you tried Brave a couple years ago and gave up, it's time to go back. If you've not heard of Brave, you need to check it out.

Brave has solutions for targeted advertising. (Google AdSense is completely blocked, and this is a HUGE deal. More on that in a minute.) Brave also has a solution for digital fingerprints. Coupled with DuckDuckGo, you can protect your browsing and searching in a way that could become extremely disruptive to information dealers in a really good way.

Let's entertain a hypothetical. Oh, come on, it'll be fun. All the kids are doing it these days. **What if everyone using Chrome right now suddenly switched all their browsing to Brave?** For the purposes of this exercise, let's assume that Brave could handle this massive scaling of its product and service (which they most certainly could not, at least from the advertising angle).

What would happen? Let's just say, not all the immediate effects would be seen as positive by many. The first and most obvious is that Google AdSense would suddenly decelerate from ludicrous-speed to somewhere around Sunday-drive. Next, widespread panic.

Google ain't gonna be happy. Digital marketers would freak. Tons of businesses would be left wondering how in the world to reach their audience.

People who have staked more time and energy into keywords and SEO would step back and sigh with relief. The sort of organic, hard work involved in optimizing search results around your brand name and keywords would continue to pay off with DuckDuckGo and all other search engines while being coupled with Brave. Tracking, and therefore targeted ads, would be crushed by Brave.

One thing you'll notice if you switch to Brave is that some sites take offense. You will receive some pop-ups saying things like, "We've noticed you're blocking ads," or "We get it, not everyone likes ads." These are polite ways for companies to hint that they rely on ad revenues, and they aren't super happy about people taking their ball and going home. Yes, many, MANY legit companies would take a revenue hit if Chrome users suddenly switched to Brave.

But the flip side of that coin is that information dealers would almost immediately suffocate or be forced to find a new host to suck dry. Sites like Facebook, YouTube, and Amazon would most likely be hit harder by information dealers looking to keep the gravy train flowing. But the reality is that too many dollars would have disappeared from the ecosystem to support the dealers at play. All but the top 10% would give up and either find a new scam or get a legit job like lobbyist or something.

At this point, it's important to state that digital marketing, and more specifically paid digital advertising, is not the problem here. I'm not saying that Brave would kill paid digital advertising. Brave actually has the beginnings of their own paid advertising system in place. It isn't by any means robust, and it will take time for Brave to scale it up in a responsible manner.

The crux of what makes Brave's advertising platform so brave is that it shifts the method by which ad payouts are determined from a conversion-based metric to an engagement-based metric. I'm hopeful that Brave fully understands this and that they are building their ad platform this way intentionally.

We'll discuss conversion vs. engagement metrics while discussing the first tenet of the Pirate Author Code in a few chapters. For now, I'll point out that clicks or views are conversion-based metrics. This is what AdSense is based on, and it is what leads to clickbait and sensationalism. The actual content doesn't need to be about what the ad states it is about. Payments are based on clicks.

At this early stage, Brave's ad platform is built to allow users to decide where the ad revenues go by where the user spends their time, i.e., by where the users are engaged. Brave uses a crypto token called BAT (Basic Attention Token). Users can earn BATs by opting to view ads. Then users can opt to reward the sites they frequent with the BATs those users have earned. In a nutshell, this would shift the main way to earn ad revenue from conversion-based friction tactics to engagement-based loyalty tactics. In other words, if you generate great content that people love, you'll earn ad revenue. To my ears, this sounds like a recipe for saving the information distribution network from information dealers.

A final word on Brave for anyone with a website, if you want to be able to receive BATs from users who frequent your site while using Brave as a browser, you must insert a line of code much like you would for using Google Analytics. This code authenticates your site and allows you to participate in the Brave advertising ecosystem.

Chapter Five

The Role of Traditional Publishers

What makes a publisher of information an information broker?

It's important to clarify that traditional publishers are not information dealers or information brokers. This clarification is a good place to interject a few standards to apply to a platform, company, or organization when trying to determine if they are information brokers or simply publishers of information.

At its most basic level, information brokers are driven by big data. The data is more important than the actual information they make available. Here are the best rules of thumb for determining if an entity is an information broker: 1) open system vs. closed system 2) free content vs. paid content 3) commodity vs. story.

Open vs. closed is a reference to the application process for information to be included or distributed throughout the platform's network. Open means that pretty much anyone can access the network with no or little application process.

Closed means the network is tightly protected by an inolved application process.

Free vs. paid content is in regards to content consumer access rather than content creator access. If a consumer is able to access the majority of the content without a direct monetary charge, well, that's free. If a consumer pays a direct fee for access to content, you guessed it, that's paid content. Keep in mind that nothing is actually free. In a "free content" system, the user is being taxed somehow. The vast majority of the time the user is taxed via advertising, but the advertising cost is paid for by the content creator.

Subscriptions can be a grey area. While a monthly subscription for internet access is certainly paid access to the internet, the content "feels free" when we are surfing the internet. The large internet providers are certainly information brokers. They've just managed the sweet arrangement of being able to charge all their users for free and open leveraged content.

Don't get me going on why internet access should actually be free and how the crushing of net neutrality is sweetening the honey pot even more for internet providers by allowing them to charge content creators and business owners via "pay to play" advertising in order to reach internet users at the same time they are charging those internet users to access the content. (Information brokering can be pretty profitable when you are able to become a double-paid public utility!) Anywho, moving on...

Commodity vs. story deals with how the platform or company regards its content. If there is more of a concern for narrative quality, this indicates less likelihood of being a broker. If commodification of the information is goal number 1, 2, and 3, well...broker they be.

So if a platform creates an open system full of free content for the purposes of leveraging that content for profit, then that system will become an information broker. Please understand that this status is not an indictment of evil. After all, no social media platform that I know of started out with the goal of "harbinger of chaos."

Big data is extremely valuable, and if a platform has created an open system with free content, then that platform will inevitably attract information dealers looking to profit from using data in an unscrupulous way.

Traditional Publishers are not information brokers...yet. Traditional publishers are neither open nor free. They are quite the opposite. Gaining access to their network is a very closed off process that typically takes great effort to overcome. And the content traditional publishers disseminate through their network is almost always (and by "almost" I mean "most certainly") monetized directly rather than indirectly being taxed via paid advertising.

Perhaps some traditional publishers wish they were information brokers, but so far none of the major players (often referred to as the big five) have unlocked how to sell directly to their consumers (or create any kind of open network that creates anything of value free for their customers). A couple of significant labels have made progress. I can think of two who stand out: Tor and Harlequin.

Harlequin has actually been selling directly to their readers for quite some time, and their website is rather robust. But, the rapid shift from print to digital hit Harlequin hard due to the smaller profit margin with digital content. As a result, they were forced to sell to News Corp and be brought under the HarperCollins roof in 2014[xviii].

One reason HarperCollins was interested in Harlequin was due to their vertical (direct to consumer) success. The big five publishers have continually shown interest in trying to duplicate this on a larger scale, but it takes serious time, energy, and authenticity to develop this kind of brand recognition and loyalty.

Tor has invested this kind of time and energy for years by providing its faithful readers with tons of interesting free content. Their newsletter and blog includes reviews, re-reads (or re-watches), and thoughtful commentary. Personally, I remember thumbing across the spines of sci-fi books in the Half-Price Bookstore of my youth looking for all of the Tor titles. Tor was the only publishing brand name that meant anything to me.

Traditional Publishing could still serve as a solution.
If one or more of the big five publishers were able to scale this kind of open community full of free content that has value to its consumers, that success would make it possible for traditional publishers to become information brokers in a manner that could prove beneficial to reading. By keeping the actual stories behind a paywall while creating an associated "fan" platform full of open and free content, it's possible publishing could find a win/win solution that protected the stories from would-be-information-dealers while providing an alternative retail platform to Amazon.

But this is a long shot. First, I'm fairly convinced the big five are not capable of scaling such an operation with enough authenticity to connect with readers. The people at the top of these companies have continued to amaze me with how disconnected they are from their own readers. You know, labeling people who read ebooks as somehow lowbrow[xix] is probably not a good way to connect with your consumers.

And yet, this is the kind of understanding displayed publicly by large publishers all the time.

Second, it's likely that even if a large publisher succeeded in creating a "direct to reader" retail platform, they would probably screw it up by running ads inside the marketplace (rather than restricting them to the open fan space), thus repeating the same mistakes of the past. This leads up to my biggest fear for traditional publishers.

The Worst Case Scenario for Traditional Publishers

The vanguards of old have weakened. Whether you cherish the days of old or wish them good riddance, it's undebatable that traditional publishers safeguarded storytelling from excessive sensationalism, misinformation, and scams for over one hundred years.

While these companies have lost control of the industry, they have not lost their power. My biggest concern is that financial pressure will lead to one or more of the big five being entirely co-opted by an information broker. To have once trusted publishing labels attached to bilge titles pitched to consumers via flimsy, friction-filled marketing tactics could prove extremely destructive for reading. Companies such as News Corp, AT&T, Google, and Facebook jump to mind. The last thing we need is further leveraged commodification of story.

There is still much to be lost when it comes to how much we trust the information we read in books. In a recent survey[xx], 35% of those participating stated that they trusted the news they read on Facebook. The rest of social media faired slightly better at 39%. Newspapers came in at 63%, radio at 66%, TV at 70%. Magazines ranked at a surprising 80% trustworthiness! Too bad print magazines are slowly dying out.

The survey didn't rank print books, because they are not often a source of current events or news. But I can promise you books are still trusted at a much higher level than social media. Part of this is due to the image traditional publishers have preserved—the perception that books (nonfiction and fiction) are high-quality, professional endeavors.

High-quality and professional aren't synonymous with expensive and snooty. Comics can tell high-quality, professional stories. The same goes for pulps, graphic novels, and genre fiction of all sorts. For the most part, over the last century, when we've picked up a book, we've expected it to be a professional product. We were confident it would be original art. We trusted it to be well thought out and to be professionally packaged. We didn't suspect it of being "fake" or being a "scam."

This kind of consumer trust has been earned, and it can be lost. Reading is already suffering enough pressure from mobile gaming and other immersive forms of entertainment that have adapted to modern technologies and lifestyles much more readily than narrative fiction has. As Pirate Authors, we need to strive for protecting the trustworthiness of narrative fiction, nonfiction, and storytelling in general.

The Evolution of the Information High Seas

In today's information high seas, traditional publishers have lost their former glory. But they still have power, and they still have value. Gatekeepers, or in this case Port Authorities, have a valuable purpose. Traditional publishers are evolving in an attempt to become more lean and more relevant port authorities for the information high seas.

Over the next decade, new port authorities will emerge with the help of smart Pirate Authors. It is my personal belief that at least a couple of the big five traditional publishers will evolve successfully enough to remain relevant. They will become important pieces of the new publishing industry as it settles around whatever new structures emerge to safeguard storytelling and the written word.

As an author, to owe one's blind allegiance to any single port o' call or to fly exclusively under the colors of a traditional publisher, even at the expense of your audience, no longer makes sense.

The modern day Pirate Author should have the awareness and wherewithal to shift their allegiance and fly whichever flag ultimately benefits their storytelling, their brand, and therefore their audience.

This is the sort of author I am advocating set sail upon the high seas of today's publishing industry. I'm openly advocating for the era of Pirate Publishing. Pirate Publishing is the best hope in our fight against the fear-mongering of the information dealers!

Should Pirate Authors use traditional publishers?

Short answer, sure. When your story and your goals align with the advantages of traditional publishing, then traditional publishing is absolutely the way to go. Flying a publisher's flag will sometimes come with benefits such as protection, prestige, distribution through vast trade routes, entry into diverse ports, etc. But there are always trade-offs of which the author should be aware.

When flying your own colors, the Pirate Author is beholden to no one but the reader. There's no escaping the reader, unless you have no commercial aspirations. The value of your cargo (your story) on the open market is always decided by the reader. A story told and published under a pirate flag has a much keener chance of being pure—of being true to itself.

Of course, that story is also free to suck, and therefore sink in shark infested waters, without any authorities insisting it remain in dry dock. These are among the live-and-learn experiences of a Pirate Author. It's while stranded on a desert island we are forced to rethink our strategy. We barter passage on a tramp steamer, we gamble in a few seedy pubs, we do the hard and dirty work until we find ourselves once again sailing the publishing seas (this time determined not to capsize and sink).

Today's publishing high seas aren't what they were fifty years ago, or even twenty years ago. What used to require the assistance of a publisher and the power of their flag for a story to successfully navigate to readers is no longer the case. What used to be a few mapped portions of the ocean has now been blown wide open to include the entire diverse ocean of readers.

The few safe trade routes have multiplied into hundreds. Available niche audiences and genres have exploded in number. Sailing vessels have technologically advanced. In other words, flying the flag of a major publisher is no longer necessary for an author to deliver a good story to an eager paying audience. But in some cases, it will still be advantageous.

Chapter Six

Stories are What the World Needs Now

Some people may ask, "Why all the fuss about information dealers to begin with?" I know you aren't asking that, but some people out there might be...so I'll go ahead and answer it. This is my book, and I get to talk about whatever I want. And you're gonna read it!

I mean, ehem, reading both fiction and nonfiction is critical for reasons I'll get into in a minute. And information dealers threaten the future of reading by 1) creating consumer friction that is contributing to the decline of reading 2) eroding the reader's trust 3) and discrediting the main retail platforms such as Amazon.

Throughout this book, we'll discuss the how and why of these three threats information dealers are inflicting on reading. For now it must suffice for me to say the threat of information dealers on reading is the largest threat facing the publishing industry, and therefore the writers and readers who are a part of that industry. The second largest threat is wrapped up with the first, and that is the publishing industry's failure to keep up with mobile technology and a relevant delivery vehicle for reading that replaces the book.

Reading is losing the battle when it comes to demanding the attention of Millennials and Generation Z. Multiple studies reveal the truth that young people decreasingly identify themselves as readers[xxi]. This is due to the lack of a relevant reading delivery vehicle for mobile and streaming content consumers. Later in this book, we'll address what a relevant delivery vehicle will look like and how one will emerge in the coming decade.

But before this new relevant vehicle can succeed, we must address the threats generated by information dealers.

If publishing is dunked in the crapper at the hands of information dealers who are wildly and irresponsibly enabled by greedy information brokers, this could be a fatal blow to long-form, narrative reading. So what? What's the big deal?

Well, my neanderthal friend, here's the big deal.

Reading and writing is how we interpret our world. Reading is how we learn to interact with truth, lies, treachery, and human emotion. Reading is how we first learn to wrestle with right and wrong. By following along with characters while they encounter any and all aspects of being human, we learn the consequences for behavior. We learn deductive reasoning and critical thinking.

We learn empathy.

Our minds are empowered as our world is expanded.

Through narrative fiction, we are thrust into new situations and given an opportunity to test the consequences. Books are life simulators that allow us to crash and burn without ruining our lives. The characters ruin their lives for our benefit! They learn the hard way so that we don't always have to.

Without quality, written storytelling our little human brains won't fully develop, and as a human race we will continue our death spiral driven by fear and hatred. But wait! We still interact with characters and story via film and television. What about my precious shows?

Written storytelling triggers brain development in a way that visual media does not. The reason in a nutshell is due to our active engagement. Written narrative requires our brains to actively participate in the construction of the story at a very high and complex level. Our brain fills in missing sights, sounds, and smells.

As a reader, we are actively collaborating with the writer. Half the work is left up to us! This means the reader has a stake in the story. The reader becomes invested in a manner that the viewer does not. The life simulation is more real due to the fact that our brains have formed so much of it on our own. Thus the lessons we learn are more real as well.

Visual media can still teach us, but the passive nature of viewing a screen and allowing the story to wash over us is entirely different from reading.

The Moral War of the Twenty-First Century

If we fail to reinvent the book in a way that revitalizes reading by making it once again relevant...if we fail to safeguard the publishing industry from information dealers, we will suffer the consequences at the largest scale and at the most personal level.

The war over control of the information high seas (information distribution network) will be the defining moral war of the twenty-first century. The weaponizing of information will certainly continue and worsen. If we cannot develop the mental capacity to accurately interpret the information we swim and sail in, if we don't develop the critical thinking skills, emotional or relational awareness to decipher informational shit from shinola. We. Will. Be. Screwed.

When I'm being honest with myself, I wonder if we haven't already arrived.

Part III: PAC Defined

Chapter Seven

Engagement Vs. Conversion

Pirate Authors Are Beholden to Reader Engagement

Over the next several chapters, we're gonna unpack the Pirate Author Code until we're elbows deep in the guts of the current publishing industry and the ideals that can safely navigate us toward a fair-weather future. So let's start with the first tenet: Pirate Authors are beholden to reader engagement. Here is the section lifted from the Code:

> We've been set up to fail because we've been tricked to gauge our success by the wrong metrics. The metrics we've been spoon-fed are for tracking consumer conversions rather than reader engagement.
>
> "What's the big diff?" you may ask...if you grew up in the eighties. Well, my fellow Generation Xer, the big diff is that conversion gauges the effectiveness of your marketing package. Engagement gauges the effectiveness of your storytelling. Which is a better

indicator of your success as an author? (Hint, the answer is engagement.)

I hate to be the one to tell you this, and by "hate" I mean "relish," but if you are generating written content and you are concerned about conversion at the expense of engagement, you are an information dealer concerned about quick payouts via spammy content rather than quality storytelling. (Oofah!)

I'm not saying you shouldn't be concerned about conversion. Of course, you can't engage a reader unless you first convert that reader as a consumer. But Pirate Authors understand that conversion metrics such as reviews, rankings, and royalties are for evaluating the effectiveness of marketing success and not author success.

For evaluating success as a writer, Pirate Authors rely on metrics such as read-through and direct call-to-action click-through (i.e., ask people to do something and track the percentage of them that do it). These metrics can tell you how much a reader is engaged with your brand.

And now for the unpacking.

An Introduction to Key Performance Indicators (KPIs)

As authors, how do we know we are a success? How can we determine if we are improving in our craft or connecting with our audience? What metric can we use to determine failure, success, and improvement? (I mean, other than how well we can hold our liquor.)

In business, we look for Key Performance Indicators (KPIs) to tell us when our company is succeeding. The trick is to ensure you are using the right KPIs. If you are tracking the wrong ones, you'll think you are succeeding, when you actually could be failing. Sometimes the difference between one metric and another seems subtle but ends up being drastic when the strategies of a company are based upon it.

As data gets deeper and deeper, new metrics become available and the ability to track them gets richer. In days of old, most authors depended on the monthly royalties statement from their publisher to indicate success. Each impossibly complicated statement boiled down to reveal exactly how much of your advance you had whittled away that month. Then you would calculate how many more months until you started seeing royalty checks.

Earning out an advance is still an indicator of success in the opinion of your publisher. But that metric tells the author nothing about the reader experience. While it is perhaps a solid KPI for the publisher, it is a terrible one for the author.

These days, things have gotten better, right? I mean, with real-time data streaming through my KDP dashboard I have mountains more metrics to choose from!

Hmmm, well, how can I tell you that the yellow liquid on your boot ain't rain?

Hunting for the Rascally KPI

Assuming the majority of your sales are generated through Amazon, let's drill down there first. If your books are not in Kindle Unlimited, your options for Key Performance Indicators are unit sales, royalties earned, number of reviews, average star rating of reviews, genre rankings, overall author ranking, and overall Amazon Kindle Store ranking. If you are in KU, then you have page reads as an additional metric to track. That's a lot of nuts!

If you are defining success by whether or not you are able to pay your bills, then finding your KPI is gonna be easy, right? Royalties earned is all you need. Nothing much has changed over the past 100 years. Now you get more control over playing around with the retail price to see if you can move more units at a lower price or make more money while selling fewer units at a higher one. But if the bottom line is net income, that can be tracked effectively. No hay problema, or that is to say, no problemo.

But, what if royalties start to drop? And this drop isn't due to anything you can put your finger on? What if the decrease in royalties payout is due to a change in Amazon's algorithms? Or due to a shift in culture? Now you're suddenly a failure, when only a few months ago you were a success. This is where KPIs get tricky.

The goal is to find a metric, or a bundle of a few metrics, that provide genuine insight into your progress as a writer. For many of us, earning a sustainable and living wage is tied up in our definition of success, but income alone is almost always a poor KPI. Royalties earned gives you no indication of your reader's experience. Royalties earned for the last month and last year tells you NOTHING about how well you are engaging your readers. And it is this engagement with your reader that will build and sustain your author brand over the long haul.

But how can we evaluate reader engagement?

The Metrics We're Spoon Fed from Amazon

Let's revisit our list of available metrics from which to choose our KPI. How about reviews? [shakes head; vomits in mouth.] Reviews were introduced as a means to improve the likelihood of a consumer making a purchase. The intent of reviews is to inspire confidence in consumers. For this reason, they are a lever for information dealers to pull, which is why Amazon has a problem with fake reviews and why authors have legitimate reviews yanked.

Reviews are a terrible indicator of reader engagement. Raise your hand if you've received a review from someone who clearly didn't even read your book. So...that review gaged that a non-reader was more engaged in your book than most of the people who read it? Is that a good thing?

Rankings aren't going to fare any better than reviews. Once again, rankings were invented to inspire buying from consumers. As a bonus for Amazon, rankings inspire competition and aggression among content creators. That competition leads to higher ad spend and more profit for Amazon. Alas, rankings are fickle. They can be manipulated by Amazon and by information dealers alike. Rankings tell us very little about our progress as writers in regards to engaging with our readers.

That leaves us with page reads...if you're willing to go exclusive with Kindle Unlimited. For the sake of this exercise, let's assume exclusivity. Page reads start to get interesting. After all, page reads are an indication of whether or not the reader actually read your book!

Well, sort of. Two things prevent page reads from being a reliable KPI. The first one is a technical problem. I don't blame Amazon for not foreseeing the mobile revolution and failing to successfully launch a smartphone or a touchscreen device. They have done a remarkable job navigating several cultural shifts and instigating some others. But their unsophisticated hardware (Kindle tablets) and their inability to nuance the extremely complicated payment structure of Kindle Unlimited have left them vulnerable to information dealer hacks such as linking to the back of the book, page stuffing, and click farms. Put simply, page reads have become gamified by information dealers.

How the Kindle Unlimited Peep Show Works

The second, and more serious, problem with page reads as a KPI has to do with the peep show system Amazon has devised via paid advertising. Yes, page reads is an indication of how many pages readers have read. But Amazon is in control of how many readers are exposed to your book in the first place. Remember all the investment Amazon has put into massaging money out of consumers? Reviews, rankings, also-boughts, ad placements, recently viewed items—everything all the way down to the ability to read content "for free" with Amazon Prime.

Amazon knows which user behaviors will prompt a purchase. Amazon knows which content to dangle where for certain levels of engagement that will lead toward more sales.

Remember the royalties statement of old? Sent through the mail by your publisher? In some ways, things never change. The metrics writers are being fed are the ones that are important to the people generating them. Your publisher judges your success by whether or not your book earns out its advance. Amazon judges your success by whether or not your content keeps readers engaged in Amazon's ecosystem (sells Amazon Prime memberships) AND generates Amazon ad revenue.

It's no longer enough for your content to contribute to Amazon customers becoming Prime members. Amazon is interested in seeing how much money content creators will pay to get the privilege of luring customers into becoming Prime members. I mean, wow. This stuff is brilliant, while...possibly diabolical.

This is how the KU peep show works. Amazon starts you out with a few page reads when you decide to go exclusive with KU. But there isn't much there, unless you drop a quarter into the slot. What the hell, you give it a go. And for a brief moment, the page reads dance! Oh, how they dance! People are reading your words!

Then the page reads stop. You gotta put in another quarter. Pretty soon, you're putting in dollars to get the same results you used to get from quarters. You get the picture.

Amazon dangles you just enough data to keep you investing in the system. But the page reads that you are able to monitor are a terrible indicator of reader engagement. They are at best an indicator of how effectively you have marketed your content for the KU environment and how well you've primed your ads. You can't ensure a successful author brand by tracking page reads. Page reads are an important KPI for Amazon. They shouldn't be for writers.

Conversion metrics are to marketing what engagement metrics are to author brand.

All of this build-up has been to reveal that unsurprisingly the metrics information brokers feed us are focused on conversion. Conversion isn't bad! But it also isn't enough. If we choose any one of the conversion-based metrics as our Key Performance Indicator, then our performance will focus on, well, conversion. And any content creator focused on conversion will smack of an information dealer using scuzzy, clickbait techniques.

While our marketing efforts should focus on conversion, the central KPI of our author brand must focus on engagement. Pirate Authors should develop short-term marketing strategies based on maximizing conversion while maintaining long-term, steady efforts to maximize reader engagement.

Holy [bleep]! You've ruined all my metrics!

Don't pretend you're surprised that I've told you none of the metrics Amazon spoon feeds you are solid candidates for a Key Performance Indicator. We've already established that Amazon is concerned about commodifying and leveraging your content in order to sell more Prime memberships. Why should Amazon care about your author brand? Why should they bother to provide you with pre-crunched metrics that indicate your effectiveness at engaging your reader?

Amazon has different goals than you. They track different KPIs. As a matter of fact, they are motivated to obfuscate the kind of metrics that would be most valuable to you. Data is money. Data is power! Why would they hand it out like acid at a Phish concert? (Man, I *am* old. At least I didn't reference the Grateful Dead.)

Not all hope is lost. There are metrics that Amazon doesn't spoon feed us, ones that we can extrapolate. At this point, the astute writer will bring up the question of read-through. (See, I knew that's where you were going next!) If you're not familiar with the term, read-through refers to the percentage of readers who finish one book in a series and begin the next. Read-through in a series is indeed a valuable metric and can serve as a solid KPI.

Read-through might be your huckleberry.

While the number of readers who initially find your book within the Amazon ecosystem is a metric that is heavily manipulated by Amazon and is an indicator of how well-positioned your content is for the Amazon ecosystem, read-through can serve as an indicator of how engaged a reader is with your author brand. For Pirate Authors choosing to sail in Amazon waters, read-through is the best KPI you've got.

Typically, the process will work something like this. Write several books in a series. Publish them via KDP. Place all the books in KU (exclusive to Amazon). Run Amazon ads on the first book in the series. Do your best to monitor corresponding increases in sales and page reads of all the rest of the books in the series. If your second book is generating sixty percent of the sales of your first, and your third book is generating ninety percent of the sales of your second...and so on, you are able to roughly gauge your read-through via your KDP dashboard.

A secondary strategy can be to create some sort of prequel for exclusive launch via KU while publishing the rest of the series broadly. Readers on Kobo will have access to book one and what looks like the entirety of the series. The hope is that some KU readers will enjoy the prequel enough to venture out of KU to purchase the rest of the series (still on Amazon), thus allowing you to primitively gauge read-through.

The major drawback of using Amazon KU read-through as your KPI is that it's still impossible to gauge the level of loyalty the reader is committing to your author brand as compared to the level of loyalty they are committing to Amazon's brand. Will they follow you off of KU? Will they even remember your story a month later? Will you be able to hook them on your next series? Or are they just churning through "free" content because Amazon waves it in front of their face when we put quarters into the machine?

This drawback is further expounded upon within the second tenet of the Pirate Author Code. And the negative impact Kindle Unlimited is having on readers is dealt with in more detail in the third tenet of the Code! For the time being,

Pirate Authors need to be aware of the risks involved while sailing KU waters. In the short-term, you will be feeding a beast that in the long-term we will need to starve.

The Best Engagement KPIs Available for Pirate Authors
The question still remains, how do writers avoid the siren song of metrics being spoon-fed to us by information brokers with very different goals than our own? If not royalties earnings, reviews, rankings, or page reads, what sort of metrics should writers use as KPIs (other than read-through)?

The answer is old-school: email list opens, email click-throughs, and any call to action engagement you can accurately and regularly monitor. If you ask people to do something for you, the percentage and number of those people who follow through constitute a powerful Key Performance Indicator for evaluating reader engagement.

Let's play out an example. If I post to my private Facebook group that my upcoming book is available for pre-order on Amazon, and I want all my fans to go pre-order now, and I track the number of people who do just that, AND I repeat the process every time I launch a new book, that's a solid KPI. The reason this KPI is better than unit sales on Amazon driven by ads is because this metric evaluates how engaged my fans are. Their pre-order of my book has nothing to do with my sales copy, book cover, ad copy, or keywords.

To be perfectly clear, in this scenario I didn't create a Facebook ad to drive people to Amazon in an attempt to generate conversions. I posted in my closed Facebook group about my upcoming release and made a clear call to action for my fans. The fans who did exactly what I asked them to do demonstrated they are engaged with my author brand.

They want my next book and they are waiting for me to announce that they can pre-order! If the number of fans excited to engage with my brand in this manner increases with every book launch, I'm doing something right!

This same kind of scenario can be executed using your email list. Using your own email list is actually recommended, but for those of you who have heavily invested in social media, you can still construct a method to track a solid engagement KPI. Create a clear call to action that can be tracked and repeated. Make sure it isn't evaluating your marketing skills. The call to action needs to target a group of people you consider fans.

That's it. Go nail down your Key Performance Indicator for tracking reader engagement and create a strategy to improve that KPI! Publishing is your high seas; own it like a pirate!

Chapter Eight

Author Brand Vs. Broker Brand, Pt.1

First, You Have to Figure Out Your Brand

There is a lot of talk these days about creating an "author brand." Raise your hand if you land somewhere between "I'm not exactly sure what that is" and "What the [bleep] is an author brand?"
Okay, I see those hands.

What exactly is an author brand?
There are times, such as when you are building an ad for a specific book, to focus on selling the book and not yourself. But the vast majority of the time, like it or lump it, you need to be selling yourself. This is the case now more than ever.

Readers most often start their search by genre and narrow it down to authors from there. Once they find an author, they chew through the backlist until it's exhausted and then they start the search over. What the reader is looking for is an author brand in a genre they want to read. They aren't looking for a book, or even a series.

Your author brand is the promise to the reader that once they commit to you, they'll receive several books (at the bare minimum) they will enjoy. Your author brand is all of the information that goes into the reader's decision—everything that communicates to them that you are a trustworthy and good resource for content they want to read.

Why do I need an author brand?

Now that you know what an author brand is, we need to clarify why you need one before we go any further.

It's not surprising that many of our author brands develop accidentally. It's difficult for us to get out of our mindset enough to experience our stories as "content for a target audience." Worse yet, some of our author brands are totally muddled and confusing, because we think of our stories as one-offs or as separate series. Why should your monster romance series affect your military sci-fi series?

Unfortunately, from the reader's perspective, your author brand is now something like "militant monster romance in space," which has a very small niche appeal. By mixing up such vastly different genres in your author brand, and failing to give the reader any means of making heads or tales of the mashup, you've lost a ton of readers. The monster romance readers can't trust that you won't spend the next year writing military sci-fi, for which they have no interest. Vice versa for the fans of military sci-fi.

By jumbling all of your content into a single, poorly-defined author brand, you've broken trust with the majority of your potential readers. They cannot trust you as an author to deliver them story after story they will be interested in. And if they can't trust you to deliver the military sci-fi they are looking for book after book, they will find an author brand they can trust to do just that.

If you still aren't convinced you need an author brand, think of it like this: What is easier? Selling a dozen individual books? Selling three different series? Or selling your author brand a single time?

Fifty years ago, it was perhaps easier to sell a one-off title. Ten years ago, the series was all the rave. Now you need a brand. In general, readers want more content, and they don't want to go through the entire curation process every time they finish a book or even a few books. They want to find an author that can deliver them days, weeks, or better yet, months of reading enjoyment.

The solution? Create an intentional author brand...or more than one.

How do I create an author brand that is right for me?

Often times, an author brand will remain squarely in a single genre. Why? This is a simple way to communicate a promise to a potential reader. You love mysteries? Great, I'm a mystery author. That's a quick connection to make with a reader, and can provide a solid foundation for an author brand.

Having said that, a solid author brand can extend outside of a single genre. One of my author brands contains weird western, space opera, and space western. Another of my author brands contains dystopian fantasy and bio-thriller. Understand that by crossing genres, a well-defined author brand becomes more difficult. But it can still be done.

In the case of my David Mark Brown western and space opera author brand, the tagline is "I explode things." The promise I make to my readers are that every book in this author brand will move quickly and include over-the-top action sequences. The stories are driven more by plot than character. They are episodic and wrap up most of the loose threads rapidly.

Whether you are reading "Reefer Ranger" based in a fictional 20th century "Texicas," or you're reading "Extinction Force" based thousands of years in the future on a planet inhabited by dinosaurs, the stories strike the same pulpy pace and tone. No matter the era or planet, my characters have tons in common. They're gritty, grumpy, and frequently pissed off at life. At the same time, they are fighting a noble cause against a corrupt system. Texas Ranger McCutchen and space Captain Jaeger are familiar, recognizable anti-heroes and self-righteous bastards. The author brand is maintained between them.

It would have been easier for me to have stuck with space operas or with weird westerns. I made the decision to go with my artistic gut on this instance. As a result, it became critical that I establish a clear and common tone in these stories. I had to develop an author brand that communicated to potential readers that all of my stories (in this brand) will deliver content they enjoy, even if they weren't looking for a western.

David Mark Brown, I explode things.
Looking for pulpy, double-barreled fiction that promises to shoot your favorite characters as much as they shoot up everything else? From the wild-west to outer space, meet gritty anti-heroes who do what it takes to get the job done. I write fast-paced episodic stories that draw inspiration from Cormac McCarthy and Joss Whedon. Enjoy the show!

This is an example of some sales copy selling this particular author brand. I have three active author brands. Each author brand needs enough content to satisfy potential readers that their risk in checking you out will pay off with enough hours of entertainment to make the search worth it. This brings us full-circle to the need for Pirate Authors to collaborate. I can't even generate enough content to satisfy most readers for one of my author brands, much less three. To do so, I need passionate pirate crews.

The author brand is one-half of ensuring you are able to unify a pirate crew and consistently satisfy your target audience. The other half is your author mission statement.

Now I have to develop an author mission statement?

If you haven't thought about your author brand, I know you haven't thought much about your mission statement. You're a business. You're a brand. To ensure that your stories are consistent in the notes they strike with your readers, you need a mission statement. This is especially true if your brand involves multiple authors.

Let's revisit my pulpy, David Mark Brown author brand. The mission statement doesn't need to be nearly as overt as the brand. In the above sales copy example, I barely alluded to my mission statement at all. But your mission statement doesn't need to be consciously understood by your reader. It simply needs to be consistent.

In this case, my mission statement is to use broken characters and broken relationships to communicate real-life consequences and hard-fought redemption. It's important to me for my heroes to do awful things and then struggle with the consequences of those awful things. I also want to portray that even the most terribly decisions can be redeemed with a significant enough cost. I believe that is ultimately what makes someone a hero—the sacrifices we make to redeem our mistakes, or even the mistakes done to us.

This gets into pretty deep territory pretty quickly. That's the point. Your author mission statement should stab at the heart of why you tell stories in the first place. Are you compelled to tell stories so that others like you know they are not alone? So that the lost are found? To provide escape from suffering?

Anywho, because of my mission statement, my stories always involve broken heroes like Die Hard's John McClain. Always. If I find myself writing a story in that author brand that doesn't include a John McClain (usually more than one), I know I'm either writing the wrong story, or I'm writing it in the wrong author brand.

Hopefully you are starting to see how establishing both the overt author brand identity AND the mission statement can ensure continuity in your promise making and promise keeping to your target audience. Once you've created a clear author brand with an underlying mission statement (and you can communicate it to others), go out and recruit a pirate crew! Then you'll be ready to rock your audience's socks off with a steady flow of stories they love.

Chapter Nine

Author Brand Vs. Broker Brand, Pt.2

This Perspective is Only Yours

As authors, we understand the concept of POV (point of view). When writing a story, the POV dictates the details we share with the reader and the tone we take. Each character in our story would require a unique POV if we chose to tell the story from that character's perspective. The reason is simple: no two characters share the same intersection of experiences, talents, beliefs, and emotions.

This is just as true in real life as it is in fiction. This is an important truth for Pirate Authors to internalize. Why? I'm gonna get a little "woo-woo" here. So if you're not in the mood for inspirational type hoo-ha about looking inside yourself then you should skip forward to the next chapter where I'm sure I'll be back down to earth.

There are stories only you can tell.

Okay, so why is it important we recognize that no two people have the same POV in real life? The answer has two parts. First, there are stories that only you can tell. Second, if you don't lean into this truth, there are stories that will never be read.

We hear all the time that there's nothing new under the sun. There is no story that hasn't already been told a million times, and we're all just regurgitating the same dozen or so stories with different spins and riffs, etc. Sure, at the most basic level there are only so many stories that can be told and they've all been told countless times (sometimes more compelling than others).

The existence of *Les Miserables* does nothing to diminish *It's a Wonderful Life*. We can love them both and enjoy them both because they present unique takes on the classic redemption story. If you were to tell a redemption story stemming from your personal perspective, it would be unique.

Each of us stands at an intersection in life that we share with no one. I stand at an intersection that includes a rural Texas upbringing, intimate familiarity with clinical depression, an internationally adopted son, a sports background, a demonic exorcism, the authoring of over a dozen novels, a love for making my own wine, a laundry list of specific failures, and a pocketful of treasures.

Each of us stands at a unique intersection.

When I tell you that I see specific aspects of this reality that no one else sees, I'm not saying that I'm particularly brilliant or somehow better than everyone else. When I tell you there are things that I understand that other people don't, all I'm saying is that I have a unique perspective.

Guess what? You do too. You stand at a unique intersection. If you've seen the movie, *Inception*, perhaps it will help to think of this life intersection as an urban landscape jutting out in every direction and dimension. You stand at the center of it. Every aspect of the urban landscape originates from inside you. The relationships, the sounds, the passions, the fears. The intersection is you.

But here's the trick. Your intersection is colliding with an infinitely complex array of everyone else's. We're not alone in this world. But the person closest to you, standing right beside you, still has an astoundingly different view.

Only you can tell the stories that stem from your intersection. There are things in this human experience that only you can know...unless you share them. I suppose this is the kernel of truth behind the expression, "Write what you know." And this is a beautiful sentiment as long as we keep in mind that writing what we know can include things we have no clue about...as long as they are rooted in some aspect of our unique intersection.

Now you gotta translate what your seeing.

Writing the stories that only you can write isn't an automatic. In and of itself, having a unique perspective isn't enough to create your classic spin on an original tale. To tell the stories that only you can tell in a compelling manner you have to take the time to understand what you are looking at. Just because only you can see it, doesn't mean you'll automatically have any clue as to what you're looking at.

This is the woo-woo part. To be a Pirate Author, you have to understand the intersection of your own life. How do your failures and successes play into your marriage? How has your upbringing impacted your spending habits? Your education, your beliefs, your prejudices?

Can you believe that there are tasks in this life that can only be accomplished by you? Are you able to accept that there are mysteries that only you can solve? No one else has the same exact perspective. No one else has the exact intersection of skills and experiences necessary to see the correct option, to make the right choice, or to put all the disparate pieces together.

And now for my personal theory.

My personal theory? Writing is the process we use to interpret the sights, sounds, and smells at the intersection of our life. By attributing pieces of our intersection to fictional characters, we gain the distance we need to play around with the emotions—to see what feels genuine and what isn't quite right. Sometimes we land on something by mistake. We strike a chord in our own gut that's so visceral it brings us to tears or it makes us laugh out loud. In that moment, we connect with an aspect of our personal intersection. We understand a piece of the scenery from our intersection that we hadn't before and our power becomes that much greater. We become true owners and protectors of a cosmic truth entrusted uniquely to us.

What about those moments when a book strikes us like this? Those are examples of an author being faithful in sharing the truth they were given. It's a responsibility and privilege of the Pirate Author to study the unique intersection of our life and then to share the pieces we come to understand—the truths that only we can know...unless we share them.

Alright. Back to the practical stuff...until further notice.

Chapter Ten

Author Brand Vs. Broker Brand, Pt.3

Pirate Authors Cover Their Assets

It's time to deep dive into tenet two of the Pirate Author Code: Covering your assets. This is gonna include everything from the debate on "wide vs. exclusive" to gathering personal information on your readers. All of it will be in the context of using your assets for empowering your author brand as opposed to empowering a broker brand.

Here is the snippet from the Pirate Author Code:

> Maintaining **ownership** of assets comes into play more with contracts and traditional publishing, but we need to be mindful of ownership when signing with Audible and other platforms as well. Pirate Authors spend time understanding rights and intellectual property.
>
> **Control** of assets deals with the two-sided coin of distribution and discoverability and includes such things as pricing, exposure, exclusivity, DRM, meta-data, and

branding. As with ownership, there may be times that giving over control is worth the value you're getting in return.

Access overlaps with ownership and control but differs enough to be mentioned separately. Think of access as the amount of information and data pertaining to your assets that you are given...well, access to. Do you know the names or emails of your readers? Are you allowed to contact them?

As writers, we spend our creative lives making assets. If commercialized, those assets will belong to someone. That someone will most likely be us or an information broker (or both). Pirate Authors fight to maintain as much ownership, control, and access to their assets as feasible in order to emphasize their author brand over broker brands as much as possible.

Pirate Authors cover their assets on as many levels as possible.

Pirate Authors have to build long-term assets for themselves whenever possible, rather than building them for others. The key for Pirate Authors attempting to empower their author brand is to understand that there are three distinct levels of covering your assets. There's plumber's crack, saggy pants, and full moon. Just kidding. There's ownership, control, and access.

The first level is maintaining the rights to your intellectual property (IP). In general this is referred to as ownership. In the specifics, it gets much more complicated than this. And I am not the guy to break it down for you. I recommend you read what Dean Wesley Smith and Kristine Kathryn Rusch have to say[xxii] about IP rights and ownership.

For the purposes of Pirate Publishing, I'll simply say ownership and rights are pretty damn important. And they are getting more so. In the last few years, we've seen the emergence of potential new rights to be licensed such as visual captioning, podcast or audio streaming, audio drama, voice-first publishing, and voice synthesization.

As a content creator, you need to be in a position to license those rights, rather than having already forfeited ownership to a broker who can now hold your content hostage.

Wait a second, some of you are thinking. You've looked ahead, and you know collaboration is a big part of the Pirate Author Code. Collaborating at the IP level means giving up aspects of ownership and control right from the beginning! Yes, this will often be the case. And sharing Intellectual Property can get tricky. But there are an increasing number of solutions emerging to help with this.

PublishDrive has released a service called Abacus that helps authors split up royalties. My company, StoryShop, is by far the best collaborative fiction writing platform available. We've combined some of the best aspects of Google Docs with powerful world-building and story-planning features.

Anywho, this leads into the second level of covering your assets: control.

Controlling your brand assets is rooted in the two-sided challenge of distribution and discovery. For authors it's a matter of distribution. For readers it's a matter of discovery. They are opposite faces of the same coin. Controlling brand assets has to deal with getting your stories out to your readers.

The easiest way to think of this second level of covering your assets is "access to eyeballs."
This is where Pirate Authors run into real problems on the current high seas of publishing. When it comes to markets, the value has always been at the bottlenecks. If a company or industry can create bottlenecks and then control them, those access points become extremely profitable for the companies that own them.

This is the driving force behind the massive amounts of energy information brokers have put into abolishing net neutrality. Net neutrality would largely hinder profitable bottlenecks within the largest information distribution network on earth. Information brokers stand to lose billions upon billions of dollars.

To best envision this problem, and to hopefully see our way to a solution, we need to approach the bottleneck as a reader. The problem for readers is not distribution. The problem for readers is discovery. The digital revolution and self-publishing movement have led to the opening up of the narrative oceans. Content is covering most of the planet! "Stories, stories everywhere, but nothing to read." Much like cable television of old, the current platforms for discovering fiction leave readers adrift and befuddled by the sheer number of options.

At the same time, readers know whatever it is they want to read next, they can find it on Amazon. Amazon has it all. While Amazon's discovery engine is far from perfect, it utilizes reviews, past purchasing behavior, and targeted advertising to help users discover the next thing to read or buy. The cost for access to all this is, ultimately, platform loyalty to Amazon via convenience and the cunning temptation of Amazon Prime membership.

Most readers, including myself, have been willing to pay this cost. This means that Amazon owns the largest access point to readers, and if authors want access to those readers, we have to navigate Amazon-controlled waters. More specifically, we'll have to battle the twin hydra heads of Kindle Unlimited and Amazon ads.

But first, let's address the possibilities outside of Amazon-controlled waters. Yes, there is a livelihood to be made without battling the hydra heads of Amazon.

Going Wide Vs. Exclusivity with Kindle Select

The first decision any author has to make when reaching their audience is to go wide or go exclusive with Kindle Select. There are numerous reasons to do either. Your asset coverage must be taken into consideration while choosing. And of course, it should be said that Pirate Authors have the prerogative to shift this up with every book or series. There is nothing that says you can't go wide with one series and exclusive with another.

First off, what type of story are you creating? Genre fiction, such as romance, sci-fi, and thriller, is widely considered to do extremely well on Kindle Unlimited where so-called "whale readers" live. (Yes, whaling is still legal for authors.) But genre fiction can still thrive on retail platforms such as Kobo and Barnes Noble, if you have the patience for it. Visually-driven content is said to have a higher chance of success on iBooks, although I've never tested this.

Geography can play a part in the wide vs. exclusive decision. While Amazon has a large share of the readership in the United States, they fare less well in other parts of the world. And while Amazon is gradually rolling out ad features across Europe, several critical pieces of their infrastructure remain available only to their American consumers (and in some cases their American content creators).

What formats are you wanting to focus on? If ebook is your main money maker, Amazon might be hard to ignore. If print is your focus, Amazon is much less necessary. If audio is going to be central to your strategy, that opens up a whole other can of scurvy. You should be aware that alternatives to Audible (owned by Amazon) are building friendly ports for Pirate Authors. We'll dig into those resources in a couple of sections.

Last but not least, a simple desire for universal accessibility can influence some authors to choose going broad over exclusivity with Amazon. While Amazon has the largest share of readers, there are plenty of global readers who choose to look elsewhere or simply don't have access to Amazon.

For more information on this important decision, I recommend you check out the Alliance of Independent Authors[xxiii]. If you choose to go wide, the next section will dig into some of the possibilities and resources out there. If it exists, I've probably played around with it. I'm only gonna mention the ones that didn't give me a rash...

So you've decided to spread your creative oats?

Remember, this second level of covering your assets is all about getting your content to your audience. Boundless means exist. Most are niche or experimental. I'm going to quickly run through a list with the purpose of priming your creative pump. It's not feasible within the scope of this short tome to attempt any sort of instructions on how to make the most of these platforms. I'll provide links and recommendations for more research when I am able.

If direct monetization is not critical to you, the possibilities expand greatly. Wattpad is a massive platform that should be considered by writers of young adult and romantic content. The vast majority of the users (in the many millions) are girls and young women. Wattpad Stars is a program that compensates the most visible writers on Wattpad, but for the most part, content on Wattpad has remained free for all.

Fanfiction sites, personal blogs, and social media are all tried and true, niche methods that have been used to publish entire books and to build traction for authors.

If you need to generate direct monetization for your content, Radish is a newer platform that originally poached many of its authors from Wattpad (including myself back in Radish's early days). Radish has attempted to expand outside of romance and erotica, but has not fared well in those efforts.

Tapas is another serial fiction service I've tested out in the past. Their reading app is beautiful and their content is curated and high quality. Mostly, their audience is graphic novels, comics, and manga.

For a couple of years, impressive effort was put into high-production, interactive reading apps. A couple of small companies are still engaged in this and have a loyal following. But overall, one-off-books-as-paid-mobile-apps has failed to take off, mostly due to the total lack of profitability for the app creators. That isn't to say it can't be done.

The Established Alternatives to Amazon Exclusivity

Now for the big dog alternatives to Amazon. The main players for ebook retail distribution are Kobo, iBooks, and Barnes Noble (...knock on wood...). Of these three, Kobo has the richest promotional environment built-in, thus making it the most direct rival with Amazon and Amazon ads. "Killing it on Kobo" by Mark Lefebvre[xxiv] is still a great resource for making the most of Kobo.

For more promotional muscle, any or all of these big three alternatives to Amazon can be teamed up with Bookbub. Bookbub is a massive email list for readers that allows authors to pay for promotional spots in emails targeted to specific genre groupings of readers. Bookbub has also started selling more traditional ad spots, mostly because of all the money they were leaving on the table from authors who can't buy their way into the promotional emails due to the demand. As far as paid ads go, these are among those that generate the least amount of friction, since everyone seeing the ads is intentionally looking for books to either download for free or buy.

There are several other large curated email lists like BookBub. There's no way I can list them all here. But Written Word Media, Book Gorilla, Kindle Nation Daily, Discount Books Daily, Book Perk, and the Fussy Librarian are all ones I've used.

Lastly, what if you are looking to maximize audio content outside of Audible? This market is evolving too quickly to keep up with. The major new player is Findaway Voices. Findaway can help you produce and distribute your audiobook without pressuring you to go exclusive on Audible.

Plus, Findaway has teamed up with BookBub's new Chirp to make a solid play in the audiobook market. Chirp combines the email list power of BookBub with a retail store for audiobooks, AND a mobile app for listening to audiobooks purchased on the platform. You guessed it, the best way to get distributed via Chirp is through Findaway Voices.

When it comes to audio, stay tuned (see what I did there?) because heavyweights such as Spotify and iTunes are making moves that could result in reshaping the seascape sooner than later. For my two cents, I still prefer streaming audio over audiobooks. Streaming an audio drama or audio story (just like a podcast) via a platform such as SoundCloud seems more in-tune (I'm killing it here) with consumer trends. Audiobooks are large, clunky files that live in non-SEO skins. But perhaps I'm reaching a bit too far into the radical future for our current purposes.

Aggregators and distributors help simplify the process of going wide.

Spreading your focus on several, even dozens, of retail outlets can be a major drag on the limited time and energy of any Pirate Author. When deploying a broad strategy, most Pirate Authors find it necessary to use an aggregation/distribution service to help.

These services allow you to enter your content, story description, pricing, meta-data, etc. and then distribute to potentially hundreds of small to large retailers. These services will collect royalties, pool them, and help you manage the sales data from a single dashboard.

While Smashwords is the grandaddy service for ebook aggregation, they are...well, old and creaky. The new players for ebooks are Draft2Digital (D2D) and PublishDrive (PD). They have very different pricing structures due to the fact that PD has shifted to a SaaS (software as a service) model and thus charges a monthly subscription rather than taking a percentage of royalties like D2D.

For Print on Demand services (POD), IngramSpark and Lulu are the main two players. IngramSpark is the independent author portal for Ingram, the largest book distributor in the game. I've used IngramSpark to publish nearly thirty titles, and their portal is getting a little cleaner every year. I would not recommend using them for ebooks, but they do a fine job with print. Avoid putting in orders around the holidays if you can. Their presses are overworked and more likely to produce defects during November and December.

Lulu has been around since the very beginning, and while I lost track of them for several years, I've recently been reunited with their services and have found them more than capable. And customer service is a huge plus for Lulu. Don't expect to get ahold of a human at Ingram. The last time I tried their customer service email it actually bounced. Lulu has also launched recent improvements in their website and user experience.

KDP Vs. Kindle Select

Even if you decide to go wide with your distribution, there is no reason to shun Amazon altogether. Tons of readers still rely on Amazon for access to content. The key distinction for using Amazon as a part of a broad distribution plan is to stick with Kindle Direct Publishing (KDP) while refraining from Kindle Select.

Kindle Select is the title for the author program that includes access to Kindle Unlimited, Amazon's reader subscription service, along with other promotional benefits within the different Amazon hydra heads. Amazon ads are still available to authors who remain outside of Kindle Select, but the full functionality of Amazon ads is restricted to Kindle Select authors only. Due to the intense competitiveness inside the Amazon ads battle-dome, it is typically recommended to enter Kindle Select (exclusivity) if you plan to incorporate Amazon ads into your marketing strategy.

Thus we've come full circle with our need to battle the twin hydra heads of Kindle Unlimited and Amazon ads. But...we're not ready quite yet. In preparation for this battle, we must consider the third level of covering your assets. We must consider access to your readers as a brand asset to be valued and protected.

Pirate Authors own access to their audience as directly as possible.

This is different from owning access to eyeballs. Level two of covering your assets, asset control, is more about the means of finding your audience and them finding you. Level three is about brand loyalty. This is so frickin' critical and yet is being rapidly undermined in the current publishing seascape.

If we remain dependent on platforms such as Amazon to reach our audience, we will continue to suffer the loss of brand loyalty as readers shift their loyalty from our author brand to Amazon's brand. Increasingly, when readers find our stories through services like Kindle Unlimited, their loyalty is to Kindle Unlimited, not to our story nor to our author brand.

Don't believe me? One way to gauge reader loyalty is to evaluate who they are more directly connected to. Who has more direct access, and who are they more willing to click a link for? Amazon customers who buy your book are required to give Amazon their name, email, and financial information. They provide Amazon their consumer habits and opinions.

They receive direct emails from Amazon about potential next books to buy.

Amazon shares none of that information with you. You have no means of contacting these readers. You have no means of providing them with additional value. These readers belong to Amazon, not to you.

But wait! Some of those consumers were sent to Amazon from my email updates! I hear you screaming. Okay, so they were willing to click a link for you. You did the hard work to build brand loyalty with those readers...and then you sent them to Amazon to buy your book. Most of us writers are willing to lend our brand loyalty to Amazon, but there is no reason for them to return the favor. We are actively working for them. They are much too smart to work for us.

Pirate Authors are going to have to help with the solution. This is a problem. The ultimate solution doesn't exist...yet. Someone needs to build a new platform that helps readers discover the content they want to read without stooping to paid advertising and sales driven rankings. The technology to do this one-hundred percent exists. But the insight, fortitude, and resources will need to unite in a corporate trifecta for this new platform to emerge. It is my hope that enough Pirate Authors will raise their flags to either incentivize such a company to emerge or to pool enough resources to create the company ourselves.

In the meantime, there are things Pirate Authors can do to ease the pain. Most of them are tried and true methods of developing reader loyalty. Things like email marketing, content marketing, social media connectivity. Do these together with your pirate crew to magnify the impact.

The key is to remember that reader loyalty is more readily built for an author brand, not a book or even a series.

Don't divide your efforts among each book. Even if you have to create stories in multiple genres, consider creating multiple author brands. Or find a way to connect the genres into a single brand.

This is where the right pirate crew is essential. Unite your efforts under a single pirate flag and create awesome stories that force reader loyalty to remain with your brand, rather than with the platform that spoon-feeds them at the buffet.

Now it's time to battle the twin hydra heads of Kindle Unlimited and Amazon ads. This is also where we begin the deep dive into the third tenet of the Pirate Author Code—Loyalty vs. Friction.

Chapter Eleven

Loyalty Vs. Friction, Pt.1

Will There Ever Be Another Harry Potter?

Not too long ago, I had lunch with a gentleman who played a significant role in the commercial success of Harry Potter while serving as an informal advisor to Scholastic. His was and is a fascinating story. With the changes that have wracked the publishing industry since the success of Harry Potter, it begs the question, "Will there ever be such a success story again?"

Or has technology-fueled social change busted up the landscape to prevent such a landmark novel from occurring? If so, is that a good thing or bad? Some of you will point to Fifty Shades of Grey as a more recent example, and while you would have a point, I'm not sure erotica has, or ever will, play by the same set of rules.

When it comes to whether broad-reaching, landmark narratives such as Harry Potter are a good thing, I think there is a much more important underlying issue. Harry Potter was genuinely a great story. It was imaginative and inspiring. And its narrative quality is what drove its long-staying and broad-reaching cultural impact. Yes, industry machinery launched it into orbit, and that industry machinery has since been dismantled. **I'm wondering if a more relevant question is, "Will great narratives ever again win the day?"** Or must we settle in with the reality that commodification of storytelling is here to stay?

There are three hurdles that must be overcome for us Pirate Authors to revitalize a publishing industry built around great narratives, as opposed to cunning (and scurrilous) marketing stratagems: 1) readers' expectations and desires are shifting, 2) narrative has been commodified and leveraged, and 3) storytelling as twisted bloodsport.

Remember my mention in chapter five of the ways information dealers are threatening reading? I promised those ways would be discussed in more detail throughout the book. Well, here's me delivering on that promise! Consider this the introduction to the three things we must do to control our author brands after we build them.

Readers' expectations and desires are shifting.

The first, and possibly most psychologically devastating, hurdle is the reader herself. I don't mean this to be a form of wrist-slapping or looking down on readers. I DO mean it as a wakeup call for both readers and writers.

The most insidious aspect of the information dealers and their impact on us is that most often we are unaware of their influence. In this case, ebooks, Kindles, and Kindle Unlimited have combined to change the way we read. The change has occurred much the same way as it has in television, video, and music. When consumers pay a relatively small monthly fee for access to "unlimited" content, we make decisions on which content to consume differently than when we are forced to sift through content to purchase a single book, movie, or album.

Our consumption of story becomes much more like an "all-you-can-eat" buffet. The single most important factor is to consume as much narrative as humanly possible. Sure, most of it isn't great, but we get a buttload of it for only $9.99 a month! You can't beat that deal with a stick!

While an "all-you-can-eat" buffet might be fun every now and then, our evolving addiction to it has lead to us being highly susceptible to the information dealers' predatory tactics. Stuff like page-stuffing and click farms have more influence on what we read next than the quality of the narrative.

Over time, we consumers become less discerning. Before we know it, our loyalty has shifted from a StoryVerse or a series or a narrative or a character...or even an author, to Kindle Unlimited itself. We don't really care what we read next as long as the supply doesn't run out. This is bad for the readers, bad for the writers, and bad for society. It's good for the information dealers that feast on the lowest common denominator.

Narrative has been commodified and leveraged.

Some of you might be wondering if this is "insidious" or just inevitable, capitalist evolution. That's a legitimate train of thought that needs to be addressed. Where the shadowy partnership between information dealers and brokers crosses into legitimately insidious territory is within the economics.

Amazon doesn't even make money on Kindle Unlimited. And Amazon doesn't need to.

Other "all-you-can-read" services such as Oyster and Scribd have attempted to compete with Kindle Unlimited unsuccessfully. Granted, Scribd is still around and still has a pretty good chunk of customers. But as a stand-alone business model, the health-club sales strategy is a losing one for reading. I've been shouting this from the mountaintops for years now. Health clubs rely on selling a bunch of annual memberships to people they hope never show up to use their services. If everyone DID show up, this would actually be bad for the gym.

This is how we want to sell books? Seriously? Can legit storytellers and publishers submit to a sales model like this and expect our industry to survive? We should not and cannot rely on a model that sells a bunch of subscriptions to readers and then hopes that most of those readers never actually do any reading.

The brilliance of Amazon is that they don't care, and they don't have to. KU doesn't have to make them money. Amazon Prime does. And any on-boarding ramp to Amazon Prime is worth Amazon maintaining. The Kindle devices, Kindle Unlimited...it's all about selling crap. And Amazon is king of selling crap. I buy crap from Amazon all the time. Who can resist?!

But as readers and writers, what we need to understand is Amazon sees books the same way it sees toilet paper and kitty litter. There is zero concern about the narrative quality of the toilet paper. Amazon isn't interested in the social impact of the kitty litter. Guess what? The people who read also buy toilet paper, and Amazon wants to sell as much of that toilet paper as possible.

The collateral impact of the massive success of Amazon is that its original pony (books) has been ravaged and nearly put out to pasture. Ebooks remain important to Amazon as the beginning of a content funnel that feeds the rest of their content desires that in turn drive people into Amazon Prime membership which ensures those people remain loyal to Amazon and thus buy all their stuff via Amazon.

The second hurdle to revitalizing the publishing industry around quality narratives is that not only has storytelling been commodified by Amazon, it's being leveraged to sell toilet paper. And nearly all of us are participating.

Storytelling as twisted bloodsport.

With Amazon's eyes on the bottom line elsewhere, the Kindle Direct Publishing arena has morphed into a post-apocalyptic thunder dome for content creators. I won't go so far as to say that KDP is an afterthought for Amazon executives, but...let's call it entertaining bloodsport. This is indeed the third hurdle to reestablishing our industry around quality narrative.

Think about this. The most influential force in publishing today is a competitive battle-sphere loosely regulated by corporate execs fixed on the quarterly bottom line. It should not surprise us that information dealers are maximizing KDP to their own nefarious ends. The most influential platform in publishing could not care less about the quality of the narrative it puts forward. Amazon is not looking for loyalty to a StoryVerse or to an author brand name. They only care about loyalty to Amazon. Only the "all-you-can-read" nature of the content, the ad spend, and the retail sales matter.

Don't misunderstand me; I'm not trying to villainize Amazon. They've simply harnessed consumer energies and utilized capitalistic machinery better than anyone else. Bezos has played his cards extremely well. My problem with Amazon's success is that I believe pure profit making, devoid of any kind of moral compass, is not the best guiding force for social good. (It certainly isn't the worst driving force either.)

This is where the importance of Pirate Authors comes into play. Our social and moral narrative must not be controlled by information dealers who are poised to dominate a profit-driven, commoditized publishing industry.

What the [bleep] can any of us do about this?
Bottom line, the stuff we read as a society can't be dominated by "all-you-can-read" garbage being proffered by shysters and hustlers in a way that maximizes eyeballs via the KDP battle-dome. The results of this type of publishing industry will be more name-calling, more "us and them" lifestyles void of empathy, more sheep to be scattered by the fear-mongering of the information dealers. More anger, more hatred, more violence. Less understanding, less perspective, less critical thinking.

I'm not exaggerating in the slightest. We need powerful, well-constructed, and entertaining narratives to reverse the shit show that has become our cultural norm. As Pirate Authors, we need to find a way to stop using ad spend as gladiatorial weapons against our fellow authors in the KDP battle-dome.

How exactly can we do this? Here is a summary of solutions, most of which have been referenced already, compiled for your convenience (and sanity).

First off, we need to not panic. Stop looking for instant payoffs at the expense of long-term success. Knowledge is half the battle, right? We need to be aware of how we are being manipulated, and we need to understand the psychology of the consumer. We need to use the system to feed the snake its own tail.

Remember to base your KPIs on engagement metrics and not on conversion metrics.

Any strategy involving Amazon should be seen as a short-term one. Understand that the time you invest in maximizing Amazon's KU payouts or product placement ads or also-boughts or category keywords or Kindle Worlds or Kindle Serials or Kindle Scout or tags or free book rankings or...(hopefully you get the point)...these endeavors are for generating short-term sales. They should not be seen as a long-term strategy.

Pirate Authors must have back-up mid to long-range plans if they are invested heavily in Amazon for the short-term.

Go wide by also targeting other major retail platforms. Services like PublishDrive make going wide much easier than it used to be.

Focus on a platform like Kobo, via Kobo Writing Life, that is much less appealing to information dealers due to its focus on books alone. Kobo is actually a pretty rich environment with promotions and opportunities that Pirate Authors can use to promote their author brand.

Pirate Authors should not neglect print. Print has the added bonus of being a safe harbor from information dealers and the constant distraction they impose on our readers. Print is able to avoid the "all-you-can-read" morass of KU. Print requires a certain devotion of attention and commitment indicative of true fans. Therefore, print sales are a stronger indication of core readership.

There are some early reports indicating that Generation-Z, folk born since 1997, are trending back toward print for books and news. This might be a temporary trend, or it might not. And don't forget about other print niches such as large print.

Along the same lines of focusing on print, Pirate Authors can choose to put time and energy into live events. Reader expos and book signings are still legitimate means of connecting with readers. With the increasing friction that digital ads are exerting on consumers, there is a renewed appeal to escape into the realm of the real. The loyalty generated by physically connecting to a reader and signing their copy of your book goes a long way toward generating a repeat customer and long-term fan.

Pirate Authors should go as direct to their audience as possible. This means continuing to put time and energy into grooming a quality email list. Communicate to your audience either via email newsletter, blog, social media, or somehow. But keep as direct a connection with them as possible. Understand that if you are communicating only via Facebook or Twitter that those platforms have control over your ability to reach your audience.

If your author brand is specific to romance and/or erotica, a platform such as Radish might be a solid option for you. These smaller, specific platforms are still middlemen, but they have little appeal for most information dealers. And if the platform is generating its revenue from taking a royalty split (or from micro-payments, and NOT from ad spend, this strips away the key lever for information dealers.

Assemble and equip a pirate crew. This is such an important and misunderstood solution I'll address it with it's own chapter (chapter thirteen) in a bit.

Finally, all Pirate Authors should be preparing for the future vehicle of digital reading that will inevitably change the game over the course of the next decade. More on that in chapter fourteen! First, let's dig into the third tenet of the Pirate Author Code—Pirate Authors grow brand loyalty.

Chapter Twelve

Loyalty Vs. Friction, Pt.2

Today's Convenience is Tomorrow's Friction

We've arrived at the third tenet of the Pirate Author Code: Loyalty vs. Friction. For nearly one hundred years, marketing efforts have increasingly been based on friction tactics. The practice of interrupting the consumer experience with advertising intensified via radio and then television. Friction-based marketing has come to a head with the emergence of the world wide web. Clunky banner ads have mostly given way to targeted advertising via Google AdSense, Facebook, YouTube, and now Amazon.

Here is the snippet from the Pirate Author Code:

> If brand loyalty is what you want, then don't be a dick. That's what information dealers are all about. If a marketing tactic feels sleazy to you, then find something more authentic to your brand.

Paid advertising is friction. This friction can be mitigated when advertising is done well, but it will always be friction.

I hear the masses crying out, "How the hell am I supposed to market my content without paid advertising!?" I'm not insisting we abandon paid ads. In the current market, it is next to impossible to find traction without them. Pirate Authors must be mindful of the friction these ads generate for their readers in order to maintain a higher ledger of loyalty.

In addition to the innate friction generated by legitimate ads, the increasing abuse of paid advertising by information dealers will increase this friction, which will in turn lead to diminishing returns for legitimate ads. So to sum up, expect increasing friction and diminishing returns from any paid advertising system.

All of this is the reason why Pirate Authors should not abandon tried-and-true methods of loyalty marketing and traction building. When done well, email marketing, content marketing, and community building generate loyalty. Popular examples include thought leaders such as Seth Godin and Tim Ferriss and companies such as Patagonia and Zappos. Connect readers with your author brand and provide them value on a regular basis.

Friction in Advertising

Advertising interrupts streaming audio and video not just at the beginning but throughout the experience! (I have no idea how this possibly works, but I guess it does.) This is the definition of friction for the consumer. Friction is generated by interrupting the consumer with something they don't want, or at least at a time they don't want it.

Loyalty is generated by giving the consumer what they want when they want it. Emails, and even text messages, are less invasive than phone calls. How huge is customer care when it comes to winning our loyalty? Print advertising is another traditional example of marketing that doesn't fully interrupt the consumer experience. Ironically, newspapers, magazines, and mailers are dying out due to the pressure put on them from digital media. And for many reasons, digital media has been superior enough for us to tolerate the annoyance of the highly friction-based marketing that has come along with it.

Often times, actions speak louder than words. Many of our favorite brands have earned our loyalty by sponsoring the activities we love, by advancing the causes we care about, and by staying true to the ideals we hold dear. These actions are especially compelling when they appear to be made in the face of purely-profit-driven alternatives that the brands are nobly able to reject.

And the purely-profit-driven alternatives are out there. They sing a sexy siren song. And they're friction based. Oolala. All of this means we're doomed to continue the cyclical dance of the information dealers. We're inundated with pop-ups, until we begin using pop-up blockers. Our phones become useless until we pay for services to block spammers and bots. Television ads dull us to slumber until we pay for a device to play back our favorite shows without the ads.

Every time we find a way to remedy the pain, the information dealers find a new way to market to us, and by "market to us" I mean a new way to interrupt our fragile sanity with consumer sirens.

Smarter Advertising Won't Save Us

The horizon of online marketing is populated with smarter targeted advertising that has the potential to pop onto the consumer's awareness right at the moment they want it. This type of advertising has already begun, and it no doubt will increase in accuracy over the next year. Here's an example of what I'm talking about.

You sign up for a writing conference in Austin, TX and then message a friend about how excited you are for the trip. You invite them to go with you. Your friend asks if the conference will be smoke free. You watch a welcome video on the conference website, but it doesn't mention smoking. You post in the conference Facebook group to see if anyone who has been there before can answer the question.

Later that day you see online advertising for hotels and rental cars in Austin, TX. They even know when you are going to be there! On Facebook, you get an add for a portable air filter for your hotel room and a mask that can filter out 99.5% of airborne pollutants and microorganisms. The next time you're on YouTube, all the ads are for writing masterclasses.

While this trend in smart advertising will temporarily reduce friction, it comes at the expense of privacy, and it opens consumers up to further assault from information dealers. With this additional ammunition and the ability to target you with specific messages at specific times, information dealers will hit us with clickbait and fake news related to the places we live and travel. They'll know even more about our tendencies and the groups we are likely to be biased against.

You're now up for bid as a non-smoking, liberal, fiction writer with anti-establishment tendencies and a strange fetish for the Dallas Cowboys. It's up to the information brokers and information dealers as to who wins the bidding. Chances are the winners are going to have nothing but profit in mind, which will lead ultimately back to friction tactics.

Amazon's Allusion of Loyalty

How exactly does all of this friction advertising translate into the world of publishing? That's the next important question to answer. After all, if I'm a reader in search of a story to read, don't I want targeted advertising to suggest possibilities? If I'm looking for a book to read, and an Amazon ad suggests a book that looks interesting to me, that's a win. Right?

Sure! As long as that book is what the ad purports it to be.

Well, you say, I always check the reviews to make sure it's legit.

What if the reviews are phony?

I check the rankings.

Click farms.

I read the free sample.

Page stuffing...after a legitimate first few chapters.

Why do you have to be such a downer!

Meh. It gets worse before it gets better. So buckle up, while we break down the reason why Amazon's apparent loyalty-generating ads are actually generating friction over the long-haul.

Consumer Data Vs. Behavioral Data

There is a key flaw with Amazon's recommendation engine. No hanky panky or sinister intent is at play here, just a lack of technology at the time Amazon built its platform. Unfortunately for all of us, including Amazon, this flaw will continue to be increasingly exposed by information dealers until Amazon's recommendation engine will either a) lose all trustworthiness for a majority of consumers (thus devastating the ability for legit content creators to reach their audience) or b) receive a total overhaul.

The key flaw is that all of Amazon's recommendations are based on consumer data rather than behavioral data.

Okay, I see those furrowed brows. Put simply, this is a difference between knowing what people have bought and knowing what people have enjoyed. And when it comes to generating loyalty vs. generating friction in marketing, these two forms of data are worlds apart.

All Amazon can determine from its consumer data is what products are selling. This is fine, as far as Amazon is concerned, because this is what Amazon wants to maximize. So when you click on an Amazon ad, the subtle reality you should be aware of is that Amazon is not recommending a book they think you will enjoy reading. They have no clue about that, and they don't really care.

They are instead recommending a book they think you will buy. Amazon's algorithms are basing this estimation on the fact you are looking at a book with similar keywords (to the ones chosen by the author of the ad) and on the fact that enough other people have bought the recommended book to suggest it is a money maker. If we lived in a world without deceit, this system would work okay. Not great, but okay. Throw a bunch of information dealers into the equation, and we get a hot mess.

For the purposes of recommendation and discovery, consumer data is flawed for a handful of reasons. What if I buy a book for someone else? What if I buy a book, but then hate it? What if I buy a book, but ultimately I'm never interested enough to actually read it? All Amazon's algorithm knows is that I bought the book. As a result, it's gonna recommend others with common keywords.

On top of this shortcoming, Amazon's system makes two assumptions that can both be extremely gamified by information dealers who are up to no good. The first is the keywords. Amazon can only hope keywords are being used accurately. They're beholden to the author to input them. Nothing prevents an information dealer from falsely using hot keywords to get their product in front of readers.

The second gamified weakness is that Amazon assumes a book's ability to be a moneymaker is based on whether it has previously made money. This circular reasoning is easily hacked by information dealers. With a quickly regurgitated story that avoids obvious plagiarism, some clever usage of the right keywords, and a bit of money for ads and a click farm, an information dealer can kickstart a spammy book enough for the algorithm to pick it up and favor it for winning the competitive ad bid. This leads to more purchases. This leads to the spammy book moving up the rankings in the Amazon store. This leads to more purchases. Now the spammy book is favored even more in the competitive ad bidding process, because Amazon wants to give the ad space to money-makers!

Let's play this out in real life.

Envision this scenario. There you are, browsing Amazon for your next read. You start with a book you enjoyed reading in the past. Or you start with a keyword phrase like, "steampunk dragon female heroine who loves the Dallas Cowboys." (Hey, it's a thing.)

Either way, you find a sponsored product ad that seems promising. You click on it. The cover looks good. The product description seems to be a fit. There are 68 reviews that average 4.5 stars. It's currently $3.99 for the ebook version. You decide to give it a shot.

You read the first several pages. So far, it's okay. Nothing earth shattering, but it's not worth throwing into the fireplace either. Then the plot starts to jump around. By the third chapter, you're pretty sure you've read a section that was repeated earlier in the story.

Wondering what's up, you go back to the reviews. You dig further into the one-star reviews, and there it is. "Don't buy! This book is stuffed with flimsy, mostly stolen and then repeated content! Why is Amazon allowing this book to remain in the store?!"

Ah, crap. Now what do you do? What can you do? First, you write your own one star review. That's at least something, right? Then you wonder how to find your next book to read...

At this very moment, the moment I'm writing this, the above scenario isn't terribly common. It hasn't yet become common enough to seriously damage Amazon's reputation or the trustworthiness of its recommendation engine. But it's inevitable that the above scenario will become increasingly common.

Amazon is losing the chess game with the information dealers who stand to make buttloads of money from immoral and illegal practices. And the baseline problem is foundational to Amazon's platform. They can only recommend books they think you will buy...based on weak data that is being manipulated by information dealers.

As it becomes more difficult for readers to sift through all the bogus content to actually find a book they enjoy, the recommendation process that used to engender that reader's loyalty will quickly begin to suffer that reader's wrath. What began as a loyalty-building process results in a whole lot of friction. Damn. And that's only the half of it.

Kindle Unlimited's short-term loyalty ends in friction. Pirate Authors also must be wary of Kindle Unlimited's "all-you-can-read," buffet-style model coupled with its "peep-show-titillation," (remember our discussion on the peep show of page reads and KU when discussing KPIs?) which is offered to authors through Amazon ads. These two heads of the Amazon hydra combine to suck authors into a cycle of building brand loyalty for Amazon as much or more than for themselves. And when creating loyalty for an information broker, there is a larger argument to be made that you're actually creating friction for your readers.

And I'm going to make that argument...like, right now.

Kindle Unlimited has been a smash hit with a number of readers. For readers who churn through 1 to 7 books a week, KU is a great deal...on the surface. But something insidious is happening beneath the surface that I hadn't considered four years ago when I started slamming the idea of buffet-style reading subscriptions (not to be confused with very targeted and genre-specific reader subscription services).

Kindle Unlimited has begun to impact how readers read, what readers read, and readers' expectations for a good story. In short, readers' standards are being eroded and worn down. This is not loyalty that these readers are experiencing. It's friction. This friction is transforming reading into a passive exercise much like television viewing. When reading becomes a passive exercise, its value has been destroyed.

This one isn't super intuitive, so hang with me. Again, on the surface, everything about KU is loyalty building. As a "whale reader" you pay a monthly subscription price and read to your heart's content. It feels like "free books!" The hurdle to trying a new book is virtually not there. Or this is how it feels.

On the flip side of Kindle Unlimited is the partner hydra head of Amazon Ads. We've already talked about how this works with typical book and ebook sales, but it's slightly different with KU because Amazon's KPI (key performance indicator) is different. When it comes to Kindle Unlimited, keeping the reader loyal to their Amazon Prime membership is first and foremost. Amazon is going to pay out for page reads at the end of the payment period. It matters not one iota to Amazon what content KU readers are reading, as long as they find enough content to renew their Prime Membership year after year.

Thus, Amazon has become good at estimating which book you are likely to read next. Remember, they don't know or care about your enjoyment. They simply need to know that other similar readers kept reading when offered this book, AND the author is pumping sufficient advertising dollars into the book. You finish one book and Amazon waives the next in front of your face. It's basically free, so why not?!

You read another. You finish the entire series...even though the fourth and fifth books were pretty slow. You're not sure you even remember reading the fifth. But the sixth got better...didn't it? Yes, you think it did. You read them all so fast.

Actually, now that you think of it, you can't remember all the books you've read this month...or much about many of them. Meh. There were a couple of good ones in there.

Much like with Amazon's recommendation engine, Kindle Unlimited initially makes it soooo easy to find new books to read. There are virtual buttloads, and even one buttload is quite a bit. This is the definition of removing friction for readers, right? Right, at first.

The Satellite TV Effect

Over time, two things happen. First, you start to find it slightly harder to find a new series or a new author. You cruise through all the content you recognize or that came recommended. You try a few new series blindly, but they aren't very good. You get through the first book, maybe the second. A friend recommends a series. You gobble that up, but once again you're left in the "series hole."

At this point, the second thing happens. You shrug your shoulders and give in to a bubble-gum series that you know won't be very good. Meh, there's eight books, and they'll keep you busy for the next couple of weeks. Once you get through them, you find another series quickly. You do this for several months before you start to wonder what has happened to you.

Why does reading feel so vapid and mindless these days? Books used to inspire your imagination. They used to keep you up at night. They used to give you life. Now they're just sucking out the hours.

Gradually you realize the extreme convenience of Kindle Unlimited combined with the commodification of the stories and the leveraging of the content to keep you loyal to Amazon Prime has ruined reading for you. What started off as loyalty-building has ended in friction! Damn, so much friction!

It's the satellite TV effect. There is such a thing as too much meaningless content. The next thing you know, you've spent an entire evening watching C-span or reruns of "I Love Lucy."

I'm not saying that Kindle Unlimited doesn't have quality content. It has tons of it. But, it has tons more of quasi-quality, ho-hum content. And Amazon doesn't care what gets read. They don't care how satisfying it is. Amazon cares that people re-up with Prime, and that authors keep a constant stream of ad money flowing. You pay, you play...and then we'll pay you.

The reader experience is peripheral. That's a problem for our industry. That's a problem for reading, and *that's* a problem for the human race. We should be concerned about the fact that Amazon's interest in selling books has NOTHING TO DO WITH QUALITY STORYTELLING. The platform that is running away with the publishing industry is not concerned about our craft.

All of us should be concerned.
Okay, now that I've made a superlative statement, I can dial it back just a little. Amazon does have one concern regarding quality storytelling. They are surely aware that if sleazy information dealers and hackers continue to run rampant on their platform, it will continue to have a negative impact on readers. And Amazon most certainly cares about the reader experience. But, as Amazon has proven repeatedly, readers are less concerned about the craft of storytelling than authors would like.

Amazon knows they can water down the quality of the content considerably and weather a certain amount of bad actors negatively impacting the reader experience before readers will object, as long as Amazon makes up for the degenerating quality with discount prices. Enter Kindle Unlimited. Enter free shipping. Problem solved...except that for authors, the problem just got ten times worse.

This is a major problem. By dominating the market and introducing elements of gamification, recommendation algorithms, and ad spend (payment for impressions) to publishing, Amazon has exposed book selling and narrative fiction to the same pitfalls that have swallowed journalism. Readers are now being fed lesser quality books from content creators who focus on the algorithms rather than the content. Books backed with enough money and the ability to play to base human emotions, such as fear and hatred (enragement is engagement!), can now infiltrate KU the same way they infiltrate our feeds on Facebook.

I'm not an Amazon hater, honest. Bezos has deftly built a strong company that has taken advantage of weak players in key markets. Kudos to Amazon. But as a storyteller and writer, I will not passively watch Amazon commodify and then leverage publishing in an effort to sell more crap. I will not simply try to take advantage of the temporary wave Amazon has created for indies. The long term effects of what is happening to stories and to readers will be devastating if left unchecked. We should see these events as a call to arms, as a call to return to the high seas as Pirate Authors hellbent on Pirate Publishing.

Chapter Thirteen

Collaboration Vs. Isolation, Pt.1

Pirate Authors Sail as a Pirate Crew

Just like that, we've arrived at the fourth tenet of the Pirate Author Code: Pirate Authors sail in crews. Here is the snippet from the PAC:

> While a pirate I be, it's not the lonely life for me. I draw within myself when I put words to the page, but I don't create content in a relational vacuum. I need my pirate crew. I think we all do. Storytelling is a collaborative process. The richer our relationships, the richer our collaborations, the richer our stories will be.
>
> On top of it all, the result of being constantly assaulted by information dealers is isolation. We are being prodded and provoked into "us vs. them" groupings in order to be targeted more efficiently by adverts. Reading and writing needs to bring us together. The only "us vs. them" we should acknowledge is Pirate Authors vs. Information Dealers.

The first task of a Pirate Author is to assemble a pirate crew.

The current "battle-dome" climate of publishing has an isolating and competition-generating effect. Even those of us whose natural inclination is to share and cooperate find ourselves being driven toward taking our ball and going home.

Unfortunately, this kind of isolation and division panders to the information dealers. People with moral complexity will never beat the information dealers at their own game. Instead, we have to come together. We have to band together as pirate crews who are able to pool skill sets, production capacity, and audience.

This can happen on several different levels. But honestly, I don't know how authors can expect to go it alone anymore. At the bare bones, authors needs a talented team of freelancers who are more than just mercenaries. An editor and a designer who know the brand and care about its success seems like the bare minimum for sailing the high seas of publishing.

Then there are the superfans or the inner circle. A few years ago, these people were called "Street Teams" or what have you. The more that these readers who are passionate about your brand are brought onto the pirate crew, the better. Establish them in a Facebook group if you must. I prefer organizing everyone on a Slack team. I think it promotes better collaboration and sense of purpose. It is a step further for people, and thus winnows the group to the faithful.

Collaboration can remain at a marketing level and find some success. For maximum results, I recommend involving a pirate crew in the creation of the stories. From the ground up, recruit a crew that shares in the ownership of the brand(s).

For those of you who think this sounds crazy, give it a moment to settle in. Author teams are emerging across all genres. Different author tribes are finding this path independently and simultaneously. James Patterson has been doing this at the highest level for several years. Assemble a crew. Collaborate on the brand. Share the booty. This leads directly into the next keystone level of owning your assets.

Content Will Increasingly Come From Well-Backed Organizations with Ulterior Motives

Pirate Publishing mandates collaboration. The forces we Pirate Authors oppose are much too organized and relentless for us to hope to succeed in our individual and divided efforts. The information dealers are those who proffer human narratives for capital gain. Via social media, journalism, and any form of media they can manipulate through paid impressions, the information dealers push fear and hatred because those two basic human emotions generate the highest ROI.

At a less diabolical but equally destructive level, information dealers feed on flabby apathy and the status quo. This is the larger threat to narrative fiction and the publishing industry due to the emergence of the "all-you-can-read" buffet model of Kindle Unlimited.

As we've already discussed, Amazon is the dominant platform in publishing narrative fiction. And Amazon's Kindle store is now fully transformed to operate via paid impressions. This means it's only a matter of time before the publishing industry is controlled by information dealers and hacks concerned more about algorithms and manipulation than with storytelling. Their influence in our lives and the lives of our readers is strong. Countering that influence requires the coordinated efforts of a trained pirate crew for the following key reasons:

1) Readers have been conditioned to expect continuous content. 2) Your author brand must publish stories with professional marketing, design, formatting, and editing (along with the professional writing!). 3) Readers have been conditioned to expect multiple books in a series. 4) Any method of gaining traction with readers that isn't based on ad spend requires the accumulation and equipping of a large audience to begin with (which typically require ad spend to acquire).

How to Find or Assemble a Pirate Crew

Finding a pirate crew isn't easy. I spent three years looking for mine. Along the way, I connected with other talented individuals who influenced my path or played a specific role for a time. But they were mostly doing their own thing and not really interested in my thing. Eventually, I found some like-minded folk through a critique group we formed. Out of that group, Fiction Vortex and StoryShop were born.

Meetups, NaNoWriMo camps, Facebook groups, and writing conferences are ways to find a pirate crew. Search your genre for other writers doing similar things. Don't be afraid to look for stuff online that you connect with and reach out via contact form or social media to say hi. Maybe it goes nowhere...or maybe it becomes a strong, professional kinship.

I'm biased, but I recommend attending StoryShop Summit (S3) with the intent of finding or assembling a crew. S3 is the official live gathering of Pirate Authors and has been tailored specifically to meet our needs. The 2020 event will be February 1-4 in Austin, TX. Permit me a small promotion. (www.storyshopsummit.com)

For all us Pirate Authors tired of short-term, friction-filled tactics, temporary formulas for success, and changing algorithms, S3 is the place to be. S3 will offer time-tested strategies from veteran authors and industry experts who have survived changing trends and shifting tactics.

S3 will assist you in finding the crew to build out your world, to keep you accountable, to celebrate with, and to commiserate with. S3 is a place to find collaborators to help you design, polish, and target your author brand. S3 will also offer introductions to partners ready to help you print, distribute, and market your finished stories.

To my knowledge S3 is the best single place to assemble a crew and the resources needed to build a brand that will survive the shifting tides of the high seas. If you decide to join us, enter the code PIRATEAUSTIN2020 upon checkout for a $100 discount on the ticket price. We want you there! And if you are reading this after February 2020, check out the website to see if there are any current or future conferences scheduled that you can attend.

Okay then, now on with our scheduled programming.

We all encounter other writers, editors, designers, etc. as we go about our business of writing. The trick is to know in advance what you are looking for in a crew. First, do you want to captain a crew or find an established one to join?

Captaining a crew involves providing direction and guidance. It involves coordination, encouraging, and correcting. Do you have the desire to bring a group together over a shared cause? To organize a shared project? Is it a must for you to be behind the helm most of the time? These things might mean you're better suited to be a Pirate

Captain. (You'll also need the ability to delegate and empower other members of the crew.)

If, on the other hand, you would rather play a specific role in a larger project, then perhaps you need to find a crew to join...or find a captain looking for a crew.

Develop an Author Mission Statement to Focus the Crew

Next, what do you want to accomplish with your writing? What's your author mission statement? This might sound like a weird thing to develop, but if you want your work to succeed, it's important to not only have a business plan, but to have a clear mission statement. Is your primary goal to teach? To entertain? To inspire? To empower? To help people heal?

We writers know that fiction has the ability to do all these things and so much more. Don't leave your storytelling mojo up to chance. Be intentional from the start. My personal author tagline is "I explode things." My brand is pulpy and fun. My mission is to empower healthier human relationships. My characters are outcasts who find belonging. I write about repairing broken familial relationships.

It's imperative that my characters experience authentic consequences to terrible decisions in order to find their way to genuine growth and healing (unless the consequence of their mistake is death). Granted, this growth path will always include explosions and over-the-top action. But the underlying mission of the storytelling is still there. Empathy and growth via circuitous effed-up paths—that's the driving force behind all the adventures of my pirate ship and its crew.

Information dealers have agendas. The narratives they push are spun to maximize their agenda and their return on investment. Pirate Author crews need to have agendas as well. We need to give readers an alternative to the base emotions of fear and hatred that information dealers most often default to if we are to redeem our industry. Figure out the driving force of your fiction—the driving force behind you and your author brand. Then go out and find / create a crew that fits with that driving force.

Equipping Your Pirate Crew

Resources for Pirate Crews are popping up. I've mentioned Slack before. When it comes to communicating with your team, I prefer Slack for direct messaging and written group stuff. I like Zoom for Video conferencing, but I know other people use Google Hangouts as well.

Of course, I'd be remiss to not mention my own platform, StoryShop. Our whole thing is to allow world building and story planning to happen large-scale and collaboratively. I've also mentioned PublishDrive before with their Abacus service that allows writers to quickly and painlessly split up royalties from collaborative projects.

Reedsy is a platform that can help you locate either a captain or crew with the advantage of knowing all the professionals on Reedsy have been vetted.

Best Pirate Publishing Practices

The more pirate publishing crews we assemble, the greater the influence we can have on the high seas of publishing. Information dealers and algorithm hackers don't have to be the only winners on Amazon. We can help stabilize the platform while we wait for alternative solutions to gain traction.

Tools, awareness, and a collective author brand and mission statement are things we can use to maneuver our nimble brand vessels around the bilge pumping machinery of information dealers. We all have access to the same tools. We may not have the financial resources or the sleazy tactics, but we can still succeed if we're intentional and we collaborate rather than isolate.

So, to recap: Find a crew by whatever means you can. Recruit collaborators and join an existing team. Be intentional about nailing down your author brand, and this brand includes your mission statement (the human element that you always come back to in your writing). Ensure that your author brand remains consistent, even while multiple authors are developing it. Use the proper tools to connect your crew and keep them working together smoothly.

Once you've accomplished all this, follow the rules of the land. Follow all the best practices of the moment. Take courses on Amazon ads, build your collective email list, etc. The main differences between your pirate crew and the rest of the indie authors out there is that you know what you are up against. You know that the rules are stacked against you, because information dealers and hackers won't play fair. You know the only constant is that there are no constants. And you have each other.

Chapter Fourteen

Collaboration Vs. Isolation, Pt.2

The StoryVerse is the Solution

More than once I've mentioned the need to reinvent the book or to revitalize reading by making it more relevant to our current technology and lifestyles. I believe a critical component of reinvigorating the reading experience is to find the digital evolution of narrative storytelling.

This may sound a bit radical, but the book (the modern-day, mass-market paperback) has run its course. We should put it out to pasture while cherishing the role it has played in our societies for the last hundred years.

Put down all your pointy objects, and let me clarify that I do not believe "Print" with a capital "P" is dead. We humans have an innate need for artifacts that represent us and our beliefs. I personally would love to revive the practice of getting cool stories in the mail, but I think the time for the print paperback book is coming to an end.

The Ebook is not the future.

And before you go there, let me say the ebook is not a replacement for the paperback. We'll nip that thought right in its cute little bud. The ebook will turn out to be akin to the eight-track or compact disks at best. Ebooks are a small, first step in discovering the future vehicle for narrative fiction and reading in general.

While I certainly will not call ebooks stupid, I understand some of the sentiment expressed by Hatchett's executive when he said as much[xxv]. I believe he meant to communicate that ebooks are not "intelligent" in the sense that a flip phone is not a "smartphone." At the same time, ebooks are not corded, dial-up phones either. Ebooks were easily an advancement for digital narrative. But just as only a few hardcore flip phone fans have resisted to upgrade to smartphones, so will the transition go from ebook to the future itiration of digital narrative fiction.

This transition will happen over the next five years as the large ebook retailers' infrastructures are outmoded and disrupted by new infrastructures. This transition away from ebooks would have happened earlier if not for Amazon's massive success in developing an entire ecosystem around the ebook. But after ten years, cracks are appearing. New Kindle ereader sales are almost exclusively replacing old Kindle devices. New digital narrative consumers are shifting to their phones for content delivery. And as we've discussed, consumer frustration with the Kindle store is rising to critical levels.

So what will the future look like?

Gird your loins. I'm dropping revolutionary wisdom left and right. The true replacement for books will need to incorporate the following six key characteristics: 1) digital 2) discoverable 3) micro-batched 4) interactive 5) bingeable 6) serial. Let's take a closer look at each of these individually. Then we'll contemplate the result of combining all six into a singular delivery method that will revolutionize and contemporize reading.

Reading Needs to be Digital

Digital is the most obvious, but it's not a foregone conclusion for many. Recent surveys have shown that readers under the age of twenty-two prefer print books over ebooks[xxvi]. But as we just discussed, the ebook is not the answer. So sure, plenty of readers will prefer print books over ebooks. What will these studies reveal once we've discovered the true digital evolution of storytelling?

The second bit of information that needs to be massaged out of these studies is that the reason these young people prefer print books is at least partially due to the fact they are exhausted by all the other forms of entertainment they consume on their mobile devices. This has long been one of my key points. Reading is losing ground to other forms of immersive entertainment that have adapted to mobile technology much quicker than reading.

As a population, we are not going to decrease the amount of time we spend being entertained by mobile devices. The amount of time spent on phones will certainly increase. The problem is that reading is not one of the top activities. Not even close. To compete with mobile gaming and social media, the new form of narrative reading must be digital.

Reading Needs to be Discoverable

In this context, discoverable refers to a couple of things. First off, discoverable means searchable. I'm talking about Search

Engine Optimization. The future delivery vehicle for reading needs to be accessible to search engines such as Google, Bing, Duck Duck Go, etc. Ebooks are not searchable in this sense. The content within ebooks remains walled off from the rest of the internet. This is even more of an impediment for non-fiction than for fiction.

Secondly, and more importantly, the future vehicle for reading needs to readily facilitate the process of readers discovering what they want to read. And this new vehicle for reading must facilitate discovery without relying on paid advertising for all the reasons we've already discussed in this book. The indie publishing boom facilitated by the internet and online shopping has introduced readers to mountains of new content—an exponential increase the likes of which even the introduction of the printing press didn't rival.

The downside of this deluge of content is the difficulty of sifting through it all to find the proverbial narrative in the slush pile. Readers need the ability to sift stories by relevance and quality in order to discover the exact content they are looking for. This is a monumental and yet essential characteristic for the future vehicle of reading.

Reading Needs to be Micro-batched

The upside of the indie-publishing revolution and its deluge of content is that now, more than ever, there are stories specific to your preferences...uh, no matter how niche your preferences are. If you want to read it, someone out there has at least attempted to write it.

And this is how it should be! In the past, shelf-space and bandwidth for publishing was so limited that available titles had to attempt to appeal to as broad of an audience as possible. Now, writers have the ability to lovingly craft micro-batches of fiction for very specific tastes. Just as in days of old we all reached for a Coors or a Budweiser (or a Pabst Blue Ribbon or Lone Star) and these days you can choose from any one of a thousand small batch, microbrews such as Moose Drool, Fat Tire, or Poligamy Porter (I'm not exposing my geo-preferences or anything...), readers can now choose between any number of sub-genre, character or location specific content. Want urban fantasy with a blind, male protagonist? Or how about alternate history in which Northern Africa dominates the rest of the globe?

The future vehicle of reading will need to feel lovingly tailored for each individual reader. The experience will need to feel intimate and personal, allowing for readers to connect with the voice, style, and content they choose to read. And writers will be smart to begin writing for and connecting with a more specific "tribe" of readers even now. Once the discoverability problem is solved, those specific tribes will seek out the narrative voices genuinely representing them and lavish their devotion accordingly. And while compelling micro-batched fiction will still find broader appeal, general-masses fiction will begin to lose its appeal universally.

Reading Needs to be Interactive

It's true, reading has always been interactive in the sense that it involves the reader to fill in the gaps of the description not provided by the author. This interactive nature, as discussed earlier in this book, is what sets reading apart from visual storytelling.

Unfortunately, new technology and shifting reader expectations have lead to a decrease in attention span for the majority of readers, myself included. Our patience for an author to weave an immersive world has decreased, and in many cases, our imagination has dulled. The sort of passive interaction required by reading has lost appeal for a shocking percentage of our population.

No doubt some of this decay is our fault, the fault of the storytellers and industry guardians. We've not safeguarded our industry from information dealers, crappy products, and shady practices. We've been slow to innovate and adapt to changing technology and lifestyles.

With all of this in mind, the future vehicle of reading will need to incorporate enhanced forms of reader interaction—interaction that takes advantage of mobile technology. The possibilities are many.

Augmented reality could allow for readers to interact with their surroundings to locate artifacts left by the author. Puzzles built into the text could challenge the reader to solve mysteries before advancing the text. Polls and votes could involve readers in future-story outcomes. Sound effects or even simple motions such as tipping the device or swiping the screen are means of interactivity that can keep a reader engaged.

For good or for bad, modern minds are growing accustomed to being awash in sensory inputs. Leaving taste, smell, touch, and hearing uninvolved in the reading process will inevitably lead to reading losing ground to other forms of immersive storytelling. The trick will be to ensure that reading never becomes anything less than reading.

Reading can be gamified, but it must never be replaced by a game. Reading can become visually enhanced, but it must never become purely image driven. The mind must always be forced to decipher the text and envision the gaps left in the narrative. That cognitive practice constitutes the uncompromisable core of reading.

Reading Needs to be Bingeable

First off, should it be "bingeable" or "bingable"? Is it just me who likes "bingeable" better? Sure, it might come across as "bing-able," but isn't that better than "bin-geable?"

Anywho, moving forward, bingeability will be required for the future engine of reading. Go no further than the evolution of television for clarity on this one. For decades, the limitations of network television required us to wait a week for the next episode.

Then came Netflix and Hulu to set the people free! It turns out, most of us don't like to wait. Or at least we want the option to watch multiple episodes in a row if we feel like it. Now most shows are released in Season dumps so that consumers can binge upon those blessed episodes! Oh the episodes! (Although, half of the magic is still the nerve-wracking wait time for the next season!)

This seems like a good time to make sure we're all using the same definition of the word "episode." We aren't referring to Uncle Jerry's recent "episode" of Tourrettes. Although, episodes, at their core, *are* centered around events. Episodic storytelling is a cyclical formula that tells a long-term story via a shorter, repetitive, and recognizable process. Each episode includes a story arc with a beginning, middle, and end even while opening up or leaving open longer-term story threads. Television latched onto episodic storytelling as its main delivery engine from its inception.

With all the love for the episodic format when it comes to visual media, why has episodic writing failed to take hold within narrative fiction? One guess. Oh come on, take a guess. You got it! Traditional publishing's love affair with the book!

For decades the book has simply made sense as a format for delivering print stories. The editorial labor and physical process of creating and shipping print books has one hundred percent dictated the mode of that delivery. For decades, we've known the recommended page-lengths for specific genres. Fantasy books can be longer than thrillers, etc. All of this has been based on the cost of creating and delivering print books.

In other words, the book has remained the main form of narrative storytelling for supply-side reasons not demand-side reasons. It isn't that readers wouldn't have loved episodic storytelling. After all, many of us have loved or still love comics, and those are episodic in nature. But for as long as the paperback dominated traditional publishing, episodic storytelling didn't make financial sense. There is no profitable means to deliver tiny, ten-thousand-word episodes in print (anymore...but more about that in the next section).

Of course, several episodes can be bundled into a single product and released as a single print book, and this has been done. But this sort of intermediate change can come across as confusing to consumers who are looking for a book but then experience a weird, episodic hybrid. While the episodes are bingeable, the book is still a single book, right? Consumers won't make the leap to thinking of the book as a season like they already do with streaming television services.

We've been conditioned to think of the book as a singular story, and a series of books as the multiple form. Due to this conditioning, we most often compare the episode to a chapter. This is dead wrong! While a chapter can be an episode, an episode is not a chapter! Remember, episodes have an arc. Episodes must tell a story to be fulfilling (unless you are utilizing the classic cliff-hanger device within a two-part episode).

The future of narrative fiction must be bingeable, and therefore episodic, but bingeable won't fly without the rest of the key characteristics in this list. In particular, bingeable content must be combined with serial content to discover the true, secret-sauce of the future of reading.

Reading Needs to be Serial

Serial is the new series. Actually, serial is by no means new. Serial fiction has been around for a long time. In fact, throughout most of the nineteenth century serial publication was the darling of the industry. Dickens and Alcott both used serial storytelling to deliver stories we now think of as classic books.

Dickens is the name most associated with the popularity of serial publication. His Pickwick Papers electrified the industry[xxvii] starting in 1836. At the time, print publication was much too costly for the majority of would-be readers to plop down large sums of money for long books. But the short installments of the Pickwick Papers were sold for just a schilling a piece.

So what's the difference between serial and series, you ask? And do readers enjoy serial installments, or have we always been influenced by market necessity? And, while I'm asking questions, aren't bingeable and serial in opposition to each other?

Whoa, slow down my knowledge-thirsty friends. The answers are ripe for harvest, but we must pluck them one or two berries at a time, lest we squish them in our grubby hands.

Series Vs. Serial

"Series" is a noun. It refers to the sequential episodes that when taken together complete an entire story arc from beginning to end. "Serial" is an adjective. It refers to a form or method of publication. Serial publication is the method of publishing a story a piece or episode at a time as opposed to collecting or finishing the entirety of the story before publishing it all at once.

By definition, serial publication dictates a shift in common writing processes. Writing serial fiction means an author must be comfortable publishing pieces of the story before the entire story is finished. To be sure, writing serial fiction is plenty different from writing an entire novel.

Do readers want serial fiction? Or bingeable fiction? Which one is it!?

As it turns out, bingeable reading and serial writing are not opposed. They are a perfect wedding. It is when the serial writing process is combined with episodic story structure that a lively dynamic emerges for the author. At the same time, readers are given more immediate access to the content they so longingly do not want to wait long for.

But do readers want their content all at once or serially released? How do we balance this odd conundrum of readers wanting to binge on an entire series, and yet readers also not wanting to wait for that entire series to be finished? How can readers possible get their serial content and binge on it too!? The answer is simple. On demand writing.

Wait. What? On demand writing? As in, writers are supposed to create content as people want to read it?

Okay, before you put this book down and write me off as a cuckoo, hear me out just a bit further.

What readers need now is on-demand writing.
When we meld together all six characteristics: 1) digital 2) discoverable 3) micro-batched 4) interactive 5) bingeable and 6) serial, something radical begins to emerge—a compelling form of intimately-customized, written storytelling available at the reader's fingertips seemingly at their beck and call. Such a reality would feel like magic, would it not? Customized, on-demand reading! More of my favorite characters right when I want them!

Is there any doubt that all six of these characteristics combined into one vehicle would revive reading on a massive scale? (The correct answer is, "No!") The trick, of course, is to devise such a vehicle which can realistically be attained by authors at scale and then delivered to readers at their convenience.

But how can such a thing possibly be done?! [dramatic music plays]

Meet the StoryVerse.
For those of you who didn't skim ahead and read the bolded headers, this moment is probably much more dramatic. Either way, the StoryVerse is the solution we seek. What is the StoryVerse? Good question.

For those of you who notice such things, you've probably been wondering why this chapter on the StoryVerse was included as Part 2 of the Collaboration vs. Isolation tenet of the PAC. Nothing we've discussed so far has had anything to do with collaboration...or has it? The answer is almost certainly, yes, it has.

The StoryVerse is a collaborative story vehicle that utilizes the collective talents of writers, editors, designers, and administrators to produce narrative fiction that satisfies all six of the necessary characteristics for the future of reading. To envision the robust and encompassing nature of a StoryVerse think of franchises such as Marvel, Star Wars, and Star Trek. Each StoryVerse contains multiple series that each overlap while exploring their own themes and settings.

The world elements such as characters, events, settings, and technologies are shared. But each series has its defining characters and settings. Collaboration within a StoryVerse can take many forms: co-writing every series, a single author per series, or author teams working within a single, massive series. Collaboration is necessary for two critical reasons, the first of which you may have already deduced—the ability to supply what feels like on-demand content to the reader.

A single writer, working alone, can't possibly write, edit, and rewrite story content as fast as a reader can read it. Five writers can. A team of writers and editors can craft better narratives while working together than they could individually. By pooling their individual skill sets, the collaborative author brand will benefit. And if each writer can generate 10,000 words of finished content a week, that's a combined 50,000 words (for five writers). That's enough content to completely satisfy many readers, providing them with an "on-demand" experience of always having another episode to read whenever they want it.

What about readers who read more than 200 pages worth of content a week? This is where the second key aspect of the collaborative StoryVerse needs to be teased out. Discovery is an energy-intensive process for the reader. As we've discussed, this process can sometimes be fraught with friction. Just as "whale readers" have opted for series over one-off books, due to the higher narrative payoff for the energy invested in their discovery, the StoryVerse would replace the series for the same reason.

Not only do StoryVerses promise several times the content of a series, they also reduce the volume of titles through which readers must search. In an online storefront, a single StoryVerse might represent ten to fifty individual seasons of story containing hundreds of episodes. Imagine this scenario: as a reader who loves supernatural thrillers, I click on the thriller genre and then the supernatural subgenre to find eight StoryVerses that qualify. Eight.

If this reader is you, are you disappointed? Are you excited? You spend a couple of minutes glancing over each of the eight StoryVerses and find two of them that look really interesting. One series in one StoryVerse looks particularly irresistible and exactly where you want to start. There is currently one finished season with 9 episodes and another season in progress with 4 finished episodes so far. That particular series will release a new finished episode every Wednesday for the next six weeks. You dive in.

After finishing all twenty episodes of this first series, you branch out and start ready others in the same StoryVerse. Before you start to run out of episodes, you start in on the second StoryVerse. Now you've got as much content as you can read for at least the next several months! By the time you finish the natural run of these first two StoryVerses, there is a new Supernatural thriller StoryVerse that grabs your attention...or maybe you'll shift gears to urban fantasy...

There you have it. The collaborative structure of the StoryVerse by its very nature simplifies the process of reader discovery. Second, the collaborative writing aspect of the StoryVerse is the only way humanly possible to generate enough content to keep up with reader demand. And by generating content that is digital, discoverable, micro-batched, interactive, bingeable, and serial…

What? Oh, right. There is still the small matter of needing the software to make all this possible. Currently, there isn't yet writing software that efficiently and fully enables teams of writers to create StoryVerses. The process requires the combination of about six different platforms along with complex legal contracts and labor intensive management.

Oh, and there's currently no reader application that enables readers to enjoy the benefits of the StoryVerse structure. These two things are true. But what did you expect? To invent a new replacement for the book and that the infrastructure to enable it would suddenly and magically appear? Nope. We Pirate Authors will have to force these resources into existence. But first, the final tenet of the Pirate Author Code: Abundance vs. Scarcity.

Chapter Fifteen

Abundance Vs. Scarcity

Pirate Authors Support the Pirate Community

Finally, we arrive at the fifth tenet of the Pirate Author Code: Abundance vs. Scarcity. This tenet is the mortar that holds all the bricks together. It's not obvious from an outside observer, but it's integral to the integrity of everything we build. Here is a snippet of the tenet lifted from the PAC:

> Pirate Authors live out of a world-view based on abundance. Creativity itself insists on a foundation of abundance. By snatching words or images out of the air, do we deplete the available stock of creativity? Preposterous!
>
> By shaping words into story, we make the world richer. And the more those stories are shared, the richer we all become! Share your maps with other ships. Inform other crews of potential hazards. We can never out-write the global demand for reading, as long as we

are working together to strengthen and protect the storytelling industry.

For the time being, paid advertising pits us against each other (as we attempt to outbid each other for eyeballs), while also adding friction to the readers' experience. But our competition is not other authors. Our competition is the information dealers and their efforts to tear down our industry by pumping it full of bilge and by polluting our reader's expectations and trust.

To succeed over the long-term, the publishing industry must find a means to connect the abundant creativity of storytelling with our abundant audience without brokering the connection with an ecosystem built on a foundation of competition and scarcity.

There is no shortage of readers.

Despite some of the things I've said in this book, the sky is not falling. Despite the decreasing number of pre-teens and teens that identify themselves as readers, there is no shortage of readers. Guess what? The human population has long been on an upward trend, and somewhere around 86% of those humans are literate. So...that's like lots of readers. With translation technology improving, we'll be able to reach a larger percentage of those readers. And once the StoryVerse comes fully online, we'll engage even more readers.

Take these numbers with several grains of salt, but in the United States there were 45,000 people working as writers in 2018 and a total population of 327,000,000. Somewhere around 50,000,000 of those can't read or don't read, leaving us with a total reading population of 277,000,000. That means that in 2018 there were 6,155 readers per writer in the United States.

The takeaway here is that writing is not and should not be a competitive sport. Readers consume content faster than writers can create it, and there are over 6,000 readers for every writer. We're fine.

Our competition is not other authors. It isn't other books. We can't write more than people can read. We are competing against other forms of digital media and entertainment. We are competing with mobile apps and social media. The more we combine our writerly efforts to bring reading back to relevancy, the more all of us win. The more humanity wins.

Scarcity Mindset 101

There is no reading quota for the average human. There is no word count at which my ability or desire to read more shuts down. There is no set number of tomes allowed for the human race and once we reach that number no more books can be written. There isn't even a limit to the amount of human waking hours that can be invested in the activity of reading before light's out. Standard scarcity economics don't apply to reading.

Scarcity economics apply for commodity-driven retail outlets such as Amazon. There is a finite number of units of kitty litter sold in the United States every year, and if Amazon doesn't sell those units, a competitor such as Walmart will. As a consumer, I don't buy kitty litter from Walmart and then find the user experience so rewarding that I decide to buy more kitty litter for the thrill. Pretty soon, I can't get enough. Scratching around in it is just so damn rewarding! And the freshness! While this is NOT the type of behavior that dominates commodities, it is the type of behavior that dominates ideas and entertainment.

Abundance and the Non-Zero-Sum

With my beloved kitty litter, the exchange of goods is an example of zero-sum. I need a bag of kitty litter. I'm only going to buy one bag of kitty litter right now. Amazon and Walmart compete by offering lower prices or higher convenience. One retailer wins and I buy my kitty litter from the winner. My money leaves my account and goes to the winner's account. The kitty litter goes from their possession to my possession. The loser has lost the opportunity to make that exchange and now must focus on winning the next.

Nowhere in this process is there every an increase or decrease in the amount of kitty litter or the amount of money. The items simply shift from one entity to another. The net loss occurs in "opportunity losses" on the part of the retailer that was not able to win my business. So...sitting still makes you a loser. This is how the zero-sum game works when coupled with scarcity economics.

Non-zero-sum is the opposite. As a writer, I work my butt off to lovingly craft a micro-batched story for my particular audience. When I share that story with readers, I don't lose the story while they gain it one at a time. Preposterous! When I share the story, I retain the wonder and love involved in creating it, plus I gain the joy of sharing it! And each reader who enjoys it gains from the passion and energy I invested in creating it.

By sharing the story with a single person, both of us are enriched. Thus, writing is a non-zero-sum game. The result of the exchange is greater than zero. Repeating this process over and over creates an abundance.

The more people start to read, the more those people want to finish reading. Reading begets more reading. The higher the quality of the reading, the more people want to read. The more relevant the reading delivery vehicle, the more people want to read. More begets more, not the other way around.

Conditioned for Competition

And yet, reversing our mindset is no easy task. Supply and demand is pounded into our heads from a very early age. And so is competition. You want to star in the game or ride the pine? You want to win? Because second place is first loser.

It's hard to pour your heart and soul into your writing and then watch some upstart land a deal that seems to be based one-hundred percent on luck not pluck. For many of us, it's natural to compare ourselves to the successes around us and either become discouraged or competitive. The only cure is collaboration and giving.

Bare with me as I get a little woo-woo once more. This mindset shift from scarcity to abundance is something that will improve every aspect of your life exponentially. Take your closest relationship as an example. The vast majority of us live out our relationships with a virtual scale of reciprocity in our minds. (This is classic scarcity thinking.) When you do something selfless and/or kind for the other person, you mentally tip the scales in your favor and hope for them to reciprocate. If they do, great! Everything in the relationship is either back to even or you feel inspired to tip the scale in your favor to see if they reciprocate again.

This sort of relationship is driven by the scarcity mindset that assumes you only have so much love and kindness to offer, and if the other person doesn't reciprocate you'll dry up and wither. They will have all the love and you will have none! (Those selfish bastards!) The first problem with this tit for tat relationship scale is that we all go through seasons in life where we already feel dried up (and seasons when we're naturally overflowing). This means there will inevitably be a time when you will do something kind for your significant other and they will not reciprocate. They might not even notice!

The second problem with this kind of scarcity driven tit for tat is that the underlying assumptions are totally false. Emotions are non-zero-sum. Sharing your kindness and love with your significant other doesn't deplete you while adding to them. In fact, the only time giving depletes the one doing the giving is when it is done out of an expectation of reciprocation.

When we live out of abundance, every kind and giving gesture we offer to others builds up ourselves as well as the receiver. Looping back around to your closest relationship, if you pour into the other as much as it takes to fill them up, eventually they will be inspired to love others as well. And instead of a back and forth, you create a spiral that continues to draw the two of your closer.

Resist the temptation to get competitive or to become bitter when life pours out reward on others but seemingly neglects you. Continue to share. Continue to give and collaborate. By doing so, you'll create an abundance that will at some point spiral back around to include you and to draw all involved closer.

Okay. That was my last bit of woo-woo (for this chapter). Now onward into the future!

Part IV: The Bright Future

Chapter Sixteen

Bridging the Gap Ain't So Hard

Up to this point, we've talked mostly about the problems facing Pirate Authors, and not so much about the solutions or positive strategies we can deploy. While the final solution, a retail platform that maintains all five of the tenets of the PAC, has yet to be realized, there are things we can do in the here-and-now to sell stories and to build an author brand that will survive the turbulent high seas over the long term.

I'm going to start at the most universal and human level before focusing in on more specific tactics. If we are deploying the wrong human strategies, then our author strategies won't succeed either. Part of this will be due to failing at life. The other part is due to the fact that as storytellers, we have to understand human motivations and relationships. We have to understand how to live if we are to nail our characters in our stories.

Living life is messy.

You've probably noticed, people are effed up. The good news? If you're willing to get messy, bridging the gap ain't that hard.

StoryShop has come forward with a call to action called #JoinTheStory that essentially challenges all of us to take back our narratives and openly explore each others' narratives. In Pirate speech, this means sailing under your own colors instead of ingesting the bilge from the information dealers about our fellow humans. From the mile-high perspective this is a challenge for us to be more human.

Take a look at it this way, if I understand what it is like to be me, great. That's a single POV upon the planet Earth at a single point in time. So...basically, I understand something like 0.0000001% of what it's like to be human. As a storyteller, this means based on my human experience alone, I can authentically connect with a tiny, tiny fraction of my audience. The more I understand what it is like to live like other people, the broader my ability to authentically connect with my audience.

To be a Pirate Author is to be a better human.
For a storyteller, #JoiningTheStory is all in a day's work. It's our job to put ourselves in other people's shoes so we can bring our narratives to life for our audience. That's the academic side of things. For some of us, academics are easy. We can study world religions. We can track Wikipedia threads all day long and then some. History. Politics. Ecology, philosophy, and economics. But how do we move past the academics? How do we actually connect with people in our real lives? In the real world? Because the more we genuinely live this life, the more authentically we will connect with our readers in the places they are living in their own lives.

This is just how it is. We can bullshit onto the page all day long, and some of us are pretty damn good at it. But it's only when we are able to crawl inside the hearts and minds of our characters that our characters will crawl inside the hearts and minds of our readers. That's when we change people. That's when we bring people closer together by educating ourselves and others to have a fuller understanding of what it means to be human.

The challenging news? Remember how this chapter started out? What? You weren't paying attention? That's right, living life is messy. But life's propensity for unpredictability is exactly why I believe we should all be yelling stuff like, "Fire in the hole!" at least once a week, or we just ain't living.

Within that adventurous frame of mind, the rest of this post will offer a few things you should consider implementing in your own life for the purpose of connecting with your audience. This is, after all, a major part of taking your narrative back from the information dealers, and that is first and foremost the task of a Pirate Author. Power to the Pirates.

Psychoanalyze yourself first.

Before you try to put yourself in someone else's shoes, it's probably smart to address your personal foot attire. Authors are more likely to be self-aware than the general populous (at least we should be since we spend so much time crawling into the heads of our characters, thus into our own). That means you're probably somewhere in the neighborhood of 10% self-aware.

Why are you the way you are? Who have been the key influencers in your life for better and for worse? What were the key shaping moments of your past? I realize these can be dangerous questions to ask. For some of us, we've blocked out traumatic past events for self-preservation. The thing is, whether we meant to or not, we most likely made personal vows in those moments.

You might have promised yourself to never be used again, or to never let someone get too close. You might have made a vow to never put your own selfish needs before those of someone else. You might have deeply internalized a false truth that you were worthless or that something terrible was your fault. You might have believed a damaging lie someone in your life spoke over you. These past events hold power over our present living—power to build up and power to tear down.

If we are unaware of the true reality of our past defining moments, then most likely we're building our lives upon a false reality—one that you told yourself in the midst of pain, or one that someone else has imposed on you through anger and manipulation. As we Pirate Authors say, "That $*% # ain't gonna fly no more," or "Not on my poop deck you don't."

Like I said before, this is dangerous mental and spiritual territory. I don't recommend you dive into the deep end of self-analysis without finding the right person to be your guide. This person might be a professional, or this person might be a trusted friend or family member. The only requirements are that they: 1) know how to listen 2) ask good questions and 3) reflect what you are saying back to you in a way that helps you deconstruct how you felt during the traumatic event and see it in its entirety with the benefit of hindsight.

Having said all that, it's important to mention that we be available to help those around us navigate through this same process. Maybe you can be the close friend and / or loved one who helps someone process past trauma in order to identify false realities and live into their true selves.

"Trips Neg D" is for you and me.

Okay, that was some deep shinola. But there isn't any way to get around the need for understanding our personal narratives before we are able to understand the narratives of others. Now let's lighten it up a bit...just a little bit.

My second suggestion for expanding your empathy and connecting with your audience is actually a company policy we've implemented. We call it Trips Neg D. That's short for the Triple Negative D Policy, or "Don't be a Dick, Douche, or Dumbass."

This policy states in a single page of text that we should respond to people in a way that will not be interpreted as being a dick, douche, or dumbass. The policy hangs on the anchors of respect and honor. I personally think "tolerance" is perfectly achievable by dicks and douches. It's an amazingly low bar that doesn't really accomplish anything. If I can disagree with you while still treating you with respect, I've accomplished something capable of making the world a better place.

Whenever you find yourself confronted with road rage or an annoying neighbor, think about the course of action you are considering. Would the other person involved in the matter most likely perceive you as a dick, douche, or dumbass based on your behavior? If the answer is yes, refrain. Find a different way to communicate.

I can hear your objections. "But they were being a dick first!" Hey, what has this whole section been about so far? If you stand on your personal belief that the other person is simply a dick, how are you going to deepen your understanding of humanity? How are you going to quash the information dealers and take back the human narrative?

Maybe the driver that accelerated around you and then slowed down in front of you recently learned their spouse is cheating on them or that a parent died. Maybe your annoying neighbor has a child out of control or is taking constant crap from a boss or coworker.

Everyone has a story. Trips Neg D is about controlling our responses enough to consider the narratives around us before we play our part in those narratives. Life is messy. We don't have to always make it messier. Take a minute to play out the story in your imagination. You know some background on some of the characters. You have keen observation skills.

The driver's car is new, expensive. The plates are from out of state. There are no stickers in the window or on the bumpers. Maybe it's a rental. Maybe they've been driving all night. They're on their way to a funeral, or worse, a high school reunion. (Have fun with it.) The point is that you've taken a long enough pause to no longer feel compelled to honk, flip them off, and accelerate right back around them.

Expand your world. Expand your narrative.

My last suggestion for connecting with other people is to put yourself out there. If you live in an area with sidewalks, use them. This is radical, I know. I'm gonna get downright weird with this next bit. Walk places. Walk places even when you could drive.

You don't have to talk to yourself while you walk, but that's how I roll. I've got a backpack that is salmon, yellow, green, blue, teal, and grey. I walk back and forth from my home to my office in downtown Nampa every day. I occasionally even waive to people or nod my head in greeting. Some people are friendly to me, and there's no doubt that I'm in general a creepy-looking, old guy walking around with a colorful backpack and talking to himself.

The point is that I'm connected to my community. I recognize it and it recognizes me. I smile at people sitting on the benches in front of the public library as I walk past. They don't know who I am, but they know I'm part of their narrative. And they are part of mine.

I know when the old, homeless guy with the long hair and camo jacket is too cold and sick to make it to his morning bench. I know how the remodeling jobs are coming along and when new people move into the neighborhood. I know where all the yippy dogs are. I know the commercial painter gets home before the electrician almost every day. The library parking garage is the best place to skate.

If the only world you know is your workplace, your car, and the inside of your house...occasionally the grocery store, then you've limited your world too much. Next time you consider grilling, eating, and/or sitting in your backyard, do it in your front yard instead. Read in the front yard instead of on the couch. Bake some cookies for the neighbors. Set up a lemonade stand (it works for my kids).

That's it. I think that's plenty for today. So get out there, all you Pirate Authors, and take back the narrative by enriching your participation in the narrative of humanity!

Chapter Seventeen

The Pirate Publishing Promise of the Future

Finally, we've arrived at the promise of the future. The last thing I want to do is blow smoke up anyone's rear (wow, that's a weird expression...er, I'm assuming that's an expression.) None of this is going to be easy, and none of it will happen overnight. Truth be told, I've personally been pouring long days, weeks, months, and years into this dream since way back in 2014.

The Incontrovertible Facts

Information dealers are damaging the publishing industry and damaging our society by eroding trust and raising suspicion.

Information brokers are fueling the fire by auctioning off our personal narratives to the highest bidding dealers.

Pirate Authors have the power to reverse the tide by coming together to snatch control of our industry from weakened empirical forces and profit-driven information brokers.

I can see some hesitant readers still wanting to push back against this last one. Yes, you in the glasses. I see that recalcitrant expression. Hey, no worries. Obstinance is a good thing in a pirate! Let's take one last look at the combined tenets of the Pirate Author Code and the impact they can have when applied by hundreds, nay, thousands of authors across the world.

As the PAC states, Pirate Authors are all about 1.) increasing reader engagement by 2.) increasing brand assets via 3.) brand loyalty tactics with 4.) increased collaboration that combine to 5.) promote an abundance mindset.

It's true, if a few dozen authors embrace the PAC, nothing will happen beyond the embetterment of those few dozen authors and their fans. But...what happens if ten percent of the professional writers in the United States, or in the United Kingdom, or in Australia, or in Brazil commit to the PAC? What if an increasing percentage of the intellectual property we writers create is well guarded and strategically developed as our personal brand asset instead of being casually pimped out to information brokers in a garish effort to gain eyeballs?

What if thousands of Pirate Authors interacted with their readers in a drastically different manner than the constant assault of information dealers? Could our engagement and loyalty tactics begin to propagate more abundance thinking and less scarcity thinking?

What if a few thousand Pirate Authors came together with an abundance mindset to share and collaborate around industry-wide solutions? I'll tell you what if. We absolutely could build the future platform for reading built around the future vehicle of reading.

The last few years have taught me that I can't do this alone. The small team I've built can't do this on our own. It will take a minimum of a couple thousand of us working together to foist control of the high seas away from the brokers and dealers who have unrightfully absconded with our beloved publishing industry.

The empirical forces have weakened. It's up to us pirates. We can no longer passively ride the algorithms and scrape together whatever booty wherever we can find it. It's time we change the rules. With enough of us, there is absolutely no reason we can't.

To succeed over the long-term, the publishing industry must find a means to connect the abundant creativity of storytelling with our abundant audience without brokering the connection with an ecosystem built on a foundation of competition and scarcity.

Here is the Deal

By my calculations, it will take 2,500 writers committed to the Pirate Author Code to establish enough momentum/gravity to disrupt the information brokers' grip on publishing and to launch a sustainable, alternative platform that establishes a direct connection between us and our readers—a platform free of paid advertising that we writers control.

Two thousand five hundred writers should represent somewhere in the neighborhood of 500,000 committed readers (an average of 200 committed readers per writer). Five hundred thousand true fans is enough to launch the future.

And the future is already underway. My company, Fiction Vortex (which includes the StoryShop platform) is not the only company committed to ushering in this future. I know of others working toward the same goal. As they publicly come forward they will be added to the list in the back of this book. Any company willing to help create the future of publishing without the need to own it will be welcome.

As Pirate Authors, this is the craziness upon which we have now embarked on together. I'm asking us to build something collaboratively and collectively. To build something that empowers author brands to the benefit of storytelling. To resist the siren song of big data and the lure of information dealing and / or brokering via the new digital frontier, the high seas must be democratized and decentralized. No single power or company should be put in a position to become the new Empire that enforces its flag to be flown over all content. We must build a federation of author brands utilizing and supporting an infrastructure that connects readers with writers according to the five tenets of the Pirate Author Code.

To be perfectly honest, and a bit uncouth, Fiction Vortex could have chosen to raise venture capital the more typical tech startup way (and I'm not saying that we didn't look into it), and then we could have attempted to build the disruptive platform I've thus far alluded to. We could have done this on our own and then attempted to amass our own information / publishing empire.

Two reasons we've decided against it. First, I think it would have failed. Second, we would have ultimately been forced to be untrue to ourselves. And that is why I believe (among other reasons) it would have failed.

We're not New York. We're not Silicon Valley. We're humble pirates. New York and Silicon Valley can't save us. Their biases and limited POV won't let them. It's up to the pirates.

Hey, we've been up against it for a couple of years already. If you pledge to the PAC, you'll be up against it as well. The seas are treacherous and shifty. And while I'm promising a brighter future, there are no time tables here. No projections.

Once 2,500 writers join the ranks of those who profess allegiance to the Pirate Author Code, Fiction Vortex will take the next step in rallying those writers toward an equity crowd-funding campaign to build the alternate platform we need.

To join us in the journey, we ask that all would-be Pirate Authors first pledge allegiance to the PAC by adding their email to the form located here:
https://university.storyshop.io/pirate-author-code/#a-6

Second, we ask that Pirate Authors spread the word about the Pirate Author Code by displaying the Pirate Author Emblem anywhere it makes sense to do so. You can use the free tool on our website to generate the watermark of the Pirate Author on any and all visuals used for marketing your content and/or brand. When possible, link interested authors back to this post:
https://university.storyshop.io/pirate-author-code/

Third, join us at S3, the official gathering of Pirate Authors. The 2020 event is February 1-4 in Austin, TX. (There will be more to follow, so check our website!) Meet the gang. Assemble your crew. Fill out missing resources required to polish and promote your author brand. Enter the code PIRATEAUSTIN2020 (or PIRATEBOISE2021, PIRATESTLOUISE2022, etc.) upon checkout for a $100 discount on the ticket price.
(https://university.storyshop.io/storyshop-summit/)

Power to the Pirate Author. #JoinTheStory #FlyYourFlag #PiratePublishing

END

Greetings from Fiction Vortex

IF YOU HAVE GOTTEN this far, we are glad to have you onboard as another Pirate Author. This book isn't typical for the kind of stuff FV Press usually publishes.

Fiction Vortex is all about episodic fiction and shared StoryVerses. We are powered by the collaborative writing software known as StoryShop (a project we have helped birth in order to spread our fiction faster!) Thus far, our StoryVerses™ have been a crazy stupid success, but our baby is still so young and frail!

It's time to suckle the milk of brilliant genre fiction until our bones grow strong enough to withstand the slings and arrows of traditional publishing's lumbering giant. At Fiction Vortex™, we are so brazen to assume we can, nay WILL, pioneer the future of digital storytelling. We scoff at the idea of ebooks being the end all of digital publishing.

Let's work together to restore the intimate bonds and direct collaboration between storyteller and audience. Let's use the technology at our fingertips to do so. Become an integral part in discovering the new balance in written storytelling—a balance forged by reader and writer together.

Greetings from David Mark Brown

HOWDILY HEY, NEIGHBORINO. I've got no idea why you're reading this little section about me, but thanks! (Unless you're researching methods of depositing digital bags of flaming poo on my digital front porch.) I can't imagine that you're interested in where I went to school, or the jobs I've had in past lives. Sure, I've done some interesting things but nothing more interesting than the stuff we write about all the time.

The stuff that really makes me tick is scheming and dreaming up solutions for today's problems. I'm also really into my family because I believe that loving families are a critical means of instilling values and dreams into the next generation that will implement and improve upon today's solutions.

I love to speak to groups and, in general, be the center of attention. If you can handle a bit of a Texas drawl and the fact that I'm a slow talker, ping me about speaking at events or via podcasts, etc. I can be found via Facebook (while it lasts) as the RedneckGranola. Same thing on Twitter. You can also ping StoryShop via contact@storyshop.io.

Peace to you and yours,
DMB

Endnotes and References

[i] https://www.tune.com/blog/year-so-far-in-ad-fraud/

[ii] https://www.cbc.ca/news/technology/youtube-advertising-demonetization-1.3755626.

[iii] https://www.trutv.com/shows/adam-ruins-everything/index.html

[iv] https://www.pymnts.com/ecosystems/2019/google-shopping-contextual-commerce-retail/

[v] https://www.theatlantic.com/technology/archive/2019/06/police-offer-amazon-ring-free-exchange-access/592243/

[vi] https://www.fiercevideo.com/video/at-t-averts-blackout-disney-deal-but-sinclair-dispute-looms

[vii] https://www.cnet.com/news/you-shared-ring-footage-with-police-they-may-share-it-too/

[viii] https://money.cnn.com/interactive/media/the-macedonia-story/

[ix] https://en.wikipedia.org/wiki/Russian_web_brigades

[x] https://theweek.com/articles/877013/how-facebook-google-are-looting-media-economy

[xi] https://www.tune.com/blog/year-so-far-in-ad-fraud/

[xii] https://digiday.com/media/revel-keeping-messy-amazons-onsite-associates-program-rewarding-risky-publishers/

[xiii] https://www.vox.com/recode/2019/11/7/20953655/facial-recognition-technology-government-fbi-aclu-lawsuit-reset-podcast

[xiv] https://www.vox.com/recode/2019/10/17/20917285/google-pixel-4-facial-recognition-tech-black-people-reset-podcast

[xv] https://www.mediapost.com/publications/article/342870/columnist-blows-whistle-on-major-sites-fingerpri.html?edition=115969

[xvi] https://www.buzzfeednews.com/article/jsvine/net-neutrality-fcc-fake-comments-impersonation

[xvii] https://brave.com/about/

[xviii] https://www.forbes.com/sites/jeremygreenfield/2014/05/02/news-corp-buys-harlequin-worlds-biggest-romance-book-publisher-three-reasons/ - 2779392d2bd0

[xix] https://goodereader.com/blog/e-book-news/hachette-ceo-proclaims-ebooks-are-a-stupid-product

[xx] https://myemail.constantcontact.com/BoSacks-Speaks-Out--On-Understanding-Advertising-Today.html?soid=1101283694210&aid=b3f397jjrAA

[xxi] https://publishingperspectives.com/2018/08/publishing-challenge-sharper-focus-less-time-reading/

[xxii] https://www.deanwesleysmith.com/killing-the-sacred-cows-of-publishing-cant-make-money-in-fiction/

[xxiii] https://selfpublishingadvice.org/go-wide-or-kdp-select/

[xxiv] https://www.kobo.com/us/en/ebook/killing-it-on-kobo

[xxv] https://goodereader.com/blog/e-book-news/hachette-ceo-proclaims-ebooks-are-a-stupid-product

[xxvi] https://www.reuterscommunity.com/topics/audience-development/millennials-killed-print-will-gen-z-revive-it/

[xxvii] https://blog.bookstellyouwhy.com/charles-dickens-show-stealing-entrance-to-serial-fiction

Made in the USA
Monee, IL
08 November 2026

68002053R00100